Praise for **Fully F**

'Another wise offering from Steve Biddulph that manages to be both practically helpful and inspiring. He encourages us to tune into our felt selves as well as to connect with a wider sense of belonging. A lovely book.'   Sue Gerhardt, author of
Why Love Matters

'Wisdom, playfulness and practicality: a brilliantly expounded way to make yourself whole again.'
Oliver James, author of *Affluenza*

'A kind and encouraging book, as well as being a helpful and essential tool for navigating modern life. I highlighted various sections and read lots of bits aloud.'   Cathy Rentzenbrink, author of *Dear Reader* and *The Last Act of Love*

'*Fully Human* gives a name and structure to something that we all experience, but mostly ignore; our supersense. As I turned each page I could physically feel a reconnection to this long lost intelligence. This book is rocket fuel to your senses.'   Andy Ramage, author of *The 28 Day Alcohol-Free Challenge* and *Let's Do This!*

'This very personal book provides great insight and depth to help us not only survive but to heal, grow and move forward with greater clarity and purpose. I loved this book and found

it enormously helpful as I continue to navigate the twists and turns of my life.'
Rosie Batty, AO, campaigner and founder of The Luke Batty Foundation

'Steve Biddulph's writing about supersense here, an intuition or gut feeling that could guide us if we were to listen more closely. In both *Raising Sons* and *Raising Daughters* Steve has listened closely to what was at the time an unconscious societal yearning for parental guidance. Today we're facing uncertain futures and an urgency to transform and Steve is back with his prescient ear to the ground; to help us with our existential yearnings and offer clues for how we can do better at being in this world.'
Rachel Ward, AM

'This book is an essential guide to what makes us human. Steve's writing is clear and beautiful, his descriptions accurate, our interior world gently laid bare. This is a book that helps us to understand ourselves, to recognise and come to the aid of others and to comprehend the profound effects of carrying on as usual.'
Dr Michael Carr-Gregg, Child and Adolescent Psychologist

'Steve has been at the forefront of helping us be better men, fathers and mothers for decades. His work has had a massive impact on millions of people around the world. With his new work he provides a concrete and easy to understand way for all of us to find fulfilment and happiness in our lives by understanding more of what drives us. We simply need to hear more from Steve Biddulph. We will be all the better for it.'
Daniel Petre, AO

Steve Biddulph

FULLY HUMAN

A new way of using your mind

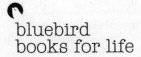

bluebird
books for life

First published 2021 by Bluebird
an imprint of Pan Macmillan
The Smithson, 6 Briset Street, London EC1M 5NR
EU representative: Macmillan Publishers Ireland Limited,
Mallard Lodge, Lansdowne Village, Dublin 4
Associated companies throughout the world
www.panmacmillan.com

ISBN 978-1-5098-8475-9

The photographs on pviii and p259 are used courtesy of the author, all rights reserved.

Further information on notes, sources and references can be found on p267–274.
The author gratefully acknowledges their reuse.

The ideas in this book are for exploring, feeling and thinking about, and they are not
intended to take the place of professional help.

Pan Macmillan does not have any control over, or any responsibility for,
any author or third-party websites referred to in or on this book.

3 5 7 9 8 6 4

A CIP catalogue record for this book is available from the British Library.

Typeset by Palimpsest Book Production Ltd, Falkirk, Stirlingshire
Printed and bound by CPI Group (UK) Ltd, Croydon, CR0 4YY

Visit **www.panmacmillan.com** to read more about all our books
and to buy them. You will also find features, author interviews and
news of any author events, and you can sign up for e-newsletters
so that you're always first to hear about our new releases.

What we think is less than what we know.
What we know is less than what we love.
What we love is so much less than what there is.
R. D. Laing

You have brains in your head.
You have feet in your shoes.
You can steer yourself any direction you choose.
Dr. Seuss

CONTENTS

Welcome

The aim of this book is to help you to move more freely inside your own mind. To 'turn the lights on' in whole levels of your consciousness that you have barely noticed are there. Once all the parts of your mind are awakened, they naturally work in harmony and you can live a more powerful, integrated and spacious life.

The book is based on recent findings from neuroscience, matched with cutting-edge psychotherapy, and my lifetime's work helping people in the worst imaginable situations to be able to heal and grow. It is aimed at literally anyone who feels that there must be more to life, and that we can do better at being in this world.

Two key ideas are at the heart of the book. The first is Supersense: the way that your body sends you messages, and is doing so *every second that you are alive*. These messages are quicker, subtler and often much smarter than your conscious brain at knowing what is going on. Yet most people totally ignore them.

The second is the Four-Storey Mansion, an easily grasped way of navigating the multiple levels of your mind and getting them to work together instead of (as they often do) tearing you apart. This method is so simple it can be learned by a five-year-old, but so profound that it can help even the most damaged adult.

The book is full of personal stories, journeys and struggles very like the ones that you might be having in your own life. But there is nothing you need to do other than be curious and read along, though we do include exercises to speed things up if you wish. It's likely that you will come to use what this book teaches every day for the rest of your life.

I hope your life is changed by it, and those changes ripple out around you, so that together we can make things better for our children and grandchildren. Loving each other and the natural world around us arises simply from realizing the connections which were always there. Your mind knows how to do this, and it's just a matter of waking it up.

With love,

Steve Biddulph

Note:

Some readers quite rightly want to know more about the author before they entrust themselves to a book. If that is you, then a few pages about my unusual life can be found at the end of the book. Feel free to go back there first if you wish, otherwise – just jump straight in.

1

Supersense

Andie Llewellyn, part-time GP and mother of two little girls, was having a pretty good day. Her parents were minding the kids, and she'd taken the morning off to go into town to have lunch with friends. Now she was headed for home. She stepped off the train at her suburban station and walked briskly, as the wind was chill, to the car park. She wrestled with her keys and bags for a moment, got the car door open, and got in. From the corner of her eye, she could see a figure in the distance, a young man moving in her direction.

As she started her car, he was closer, and calling something to her. He was well dressed, quite nice looking, it seemed he wanted her help with something – maybe he had lost something or needed directions? Her lifelong habit of good manners tugged at her conscience; it went against the grain to ignore someone. Her hand even went to the window to wind it down. But somewhere in the pit of her stomach a tiny clenching sensation made itself felt, and uncharacteristically, almost in a panic, she drove quickly past him and out onto the road. In the mirror, she saw him standing, motionless, staring after her.

Even when she got home, her heart was still pounding. What's the matter with me? she thought.

Back in the tumult of home, the warm greetings of her parents and her little daughters, Andie pushed the incident out of her mind. Until she watched that night's TV news. A man had been arrested by the police near a suburban train station – *her train station*. He had attempted to abduct a young woman at knife-point, but she had screamed and fought back, and, by incredible good luck, two other women had driven into the car park just then and the man had fled. Andie's mind took just a few seconds to make the connection – *it had almost been her*. And that poor other woman . . . Andie's husband was shocked, coming into the living room, to find her shaking and sobbing on the couch.

Together, they rang the police. That night, two detectives came to her house, they brought photographs. She was able to identify the man as the one who had approached her car. They thanked her and said that she was very smart to have avoided him. (They carefully did not use the word 'escaped'.) Andie was shivering and shaking again as her husband saw the detectives to the door.

Andie was a patient of mine when I was starting out as a young therapist. She stayed safe and, quite possibly, alive on that windy afternoon because she listened to some very specific signals – literally, her 'gut feelings'. She reacted in exactly the way that she needed to, to protect her own life. This was a wired-in response of the kind that has kept people alive for millennia.

In our species' long prehistory, there were always dangers, and we needed highly tuned senses to stay safe. A sudden quietening of the birds, a flicker of movement through the trees – we reacted first, and then our brain got going to figure out what to do next. Hide, run, call out a warning. Or just relax and say, 'Welcome home!'

Our brains are very good at this; information coming in through our senses is processed and assessed almost instantly, long before we have time to think or reason. This is your supersense, and it adds up complicated and subtle information to determine what is important for you to notice. It is doing this every second of every day. Before neuroscience properly explained this, it would have been called 'intuition' or a 'sixth sense', but it's neither. It's a very advanced capacity that your brain has, firstly to integrate sensory information at lightning speed, then to run this past the accumulated memory of your whole lifetime, to see if it 'rings a bell'. Your supersense then performs its third miracle – *it lets you know*. It triggers bodily changes strong enough to alert you – again, faster than words – that this is urgent. And if, like Andie, you are aware, 'in touch' with your insides, you will get the message.

We modern humans have been told, in myriad direct and indirect ways, that our brain is the smartest part of us. By 'brain' we mean the thin orange rind of our brain (the prefrontal cortex) that's involved in conscious verbal thinking, the part that deals with everything from 'Did I lock the door?' to 'Should I get Netflix?' That part of our brain is impressive, but compared to our supersense it's a plodding infant. Your supersense is so profoundly capable that understanding it will knock your socks off, though we are getting ahead of ourselves here – we've got a whole book ahead of us. You have this supersense, and in the course of reading these pages you will learn to apply it to higher and higher levels of your life. Alone or with family, at work, with friends and out in the world. It is always there, not just to keep you safe, but to inform your choices and maximize your happiness in life. You have a guidance system that is superb, subtle and powerful, and this book will teach you to use it.

We Almost Lost It

Our internal sensory system is the very core of our humanness, of how our mind is designed to work. So it's rather shocking that, in the modern world, we have forgotten that these senses exist. We haven't been encouraged in childhood to listen to them and we don't even have the language to talk about them. Most people are dimly aware of inner warning signals – disquiet or misgivings; or the positive ones – urgings or yearnings – but we mostly ignore them. This is no small thing; without this information, we may well live a life that is full of blunders, large and small. We might marry the wrong person, choose the wrong

Without our supersense . . . we might marry the wrong person, choose the wrong career, miss some warning sign in one of our children that turns out to really matter. Or we just volunteer for the sausage sizzle fundraiser when we really shouldn't have!

career, miss some warning sign in one of our children that turns out to really matter. Or we just volunteer for the sausage sizzle fundraiser when we really shouldn't have!

Our supersense evolved to be our mind's primary guidance system, our brain's way of knowing what is right or wrong for us, safe or unsafe. If we lose touch with it, a whole cascade of things can go wrong. We won't have a strong sense of self – of who we are or what we want. We may start to lose our way in relationships and find our family unravelling. Ignoring inner misgivings, we may lose touch with our values, and soon we feel that we are living a lie, that we've become just a collection of cliches and poses. We have no power or authenticity in anything we do. Does any of this sound familiar?

If this applies to you, then this book brings a message of hope: if you are struggling in any area of your life, that is something that can change. You can reawaken your supersense and begin to know who you are and what matters to you, and bring wholeness back into your life again. Your life can be so much more. If you are doubtful that this is true, let me present some evidence that you can check out.

In the course of your life, you have almost certainly encountered people who seemed different and special, in a good way. Much more alive and more real than those around them. We all notice such people; in fact, we supersense them from the very first, and the evidence bears it out over time.

Such people often have three distinct qualities. First, their bearing – they seem grounded and unhurried, their attention is focused, and they are right with you, here and now. Second, their manner – they take themselves and life's ups and downs lightly, but at the same time they can be strikingly fierce and grave when it really matters. They are protective of others, and the world. You feel very safe with them. And thirdly, they are non-conformist; they may get along well with others, but they don't live by the usual norms. They are true to themselves and don't simply dance to society's crazy tune.

A person who is 'fully human' stands out from the crowd. Such individuals seem to function on a more integrated level. Heart, head and spirit are going in the same direction.

What brain science is discovering is that this kind of aliveness is a neurological state – of *having more of your mental faculties activated* – and that it is available to all of us. Supersense is the beginning, the core where personhood begins. Once you can read your supersense, you can then move upwards to emotions, to thought and to a feeling of connection with everything around you. Your consciousness is like a mansion with many floors, and you can open up all the rooms and enjoy what they have to offer. With your faculties switched on like this, you will automatically start to become more integrated; the contradictions between feelings, action and values will start to disappear. You will be and feel whole.

What this book will teach you involves paying attention in some new ways, but it is not complicated – even a five-year-old child can master it. This is a set of tools to use for the rest of your life, and you will find that it makes a difference from the first day that you start.

It's Not Just About Danger

The origins of our supersense lie deep in our prehistory. We humans didn't show a lot of promise in our early days, skulking about on the savannah, cracking the marrowbones left by lions, or sucking on shellfish on the shores of African lakes.

We had the same acute senses and highly tuned nervous system as a leopard or a wedge-tailed eagle, but we didn't have claws or fangs, and we weren't especially strong or large. Our place on the food chain could have been rather low (i.e. we would have been food!), but there was one thing going for us: it was the skill that was to take us – literally – to the stars. This ability was the key to everything humans have done – medicine, art, music, tandoori-chicken pies. We *Homo sapiens* are the ultimate cooperators. Our species survived and mastered our world by living and working in tight-knit family groups, who cared for and protected each other; at least, most of the time. Alone, we were puny, but, as many a cave bear learned to its dismay, if you took on one human, you took on the whole clan.

Working together takes a lot of coordination and social skill. So, even before we had words, we had to know how to read each other well, avoid conflict, soothe fears or tensions. We are the only animal to have the whites of our eyes visible all the time, so we can follow the direction of each other's gaze. We have a wider range of emotional facial expressions than any other creature. This helps us gauge each other's mood, both to minimize dangerous flare-ups, but also to create intimacy and have fun, which are very bonding. We are a creative, playful and loving species, too. One of the things that often strikes visitors to hunter-gatherer or other indigenous societies is the warmth, exuberance and natural affection that people show. (This was absolutely my experience in Papua New Guinea in the 1970s. It's commented on repeatedly in *The Continuum Concept* – Jean Liedloff's classic book on Amazonian tribal parenting). It's been noted for as long as the West has encountered the pre-industrial world – these cultures make contemporary city dwellers look like uptight zombies by comparison. They have something we have lost.

Today, we still use the lightning-fast brain-processing that Andie relied on to read tiny signals in the body language of others, their facial changes, turns of phrase, little things that don't add up. So we know when our child is bothered about something, or is not telling us the whole truth. When our partner is keeping something from us – even if it's just a birthday surprise! When a business deal or arrangement might not be all that it appears. This signalling system came long before humans had words. So the language of our supersense *is visceral, not verbal.* It might be your stomach, your jaw, your shoulder muscles, your intestines, your genitals – literally anywhere in your body. If you want to find your 'gut feelings', just send your attention out into your body, especially down its midline – your heart, your digestive tract – but it can be anywhere, as *there will always be something going on.* Even happiness has a gut feeling.

How does it work? All day, every day, your senses take in vast amounts of information, far more than you can consciously pay attention to. Deep in your brain, these are cross-checked automatically with your lifetime memories. Then something remarkable happens. Your hippocampus (where your memories live) talks to your amygdala (where your emotions live) and sends signals down your vagus nerve (actually a vast network of nerves to your many organs and beyond). All that you know about this is that a physical something happens, suddenly, somewhere, in your gut, your scalp, your shoulder muscles, in the muscles around your heart, or even in your hands or feet, which alerts you that your unconscious brain has something to tell you.

Parts of your body activate and your conscious mind can notice them, question them. What is it? What is wrong? It's an extraordinary power just waiting to be used. A twinge in your stomach can be there for years, around a particular topic or aspect of your life, then one day you ask it what it's about, and it tells you.

The collaboration between your limbic system (which is completely non-verbal) and all the other preconscious parts of your brain is identical to that of our animal cousins – we have the alertness and instincts of a fox or an eagle, but we also have a neocortex that can think and reason. We have to bring both of those together.

Supersense never stops, even when we are asleep. It doesn't just deal with the outer world; our inner thoughts and ideas affect it too. I am sure you've experienced this – a feeling that just 'niggles' (such a lovely word) and won't go away. It can happen in just minutes, or it can build up over years. Something isn't right. And then, one day, the message breaks through to our rational, verbal mind:

This friend is not a friend.
I am not taking my child back to that carer.
This job is not for me.
My marriage is unsafe and disrespectful, and I will no longer
accept that.

Over the years, so many instances of this have been told to me. This one is especially poignant. A friend of mine, now in her late forties, developed a migraine three months into her marriage and suffered from it for almost twenty years. Then, one day, she discovered that her husband had a lover, he had started the affair soon after their marriage. Within weeks of making the discovery, shocked and betrayed, she separated from him. The migraines stopped and have never returned.

Our bodies are amazing things, and they talk to us all the time. If we don't listen, then they have to shout. Eventually, your slowpoke conscious brain comes online and you work out the next steps you have to take. But first you had to be woken up.

Does It Always Work?

It's important to say here that this sensory processing system is not infallible, and getting your logical brain into gear quickly is still important. Your alarm system can be contaminated by past experiences that are actually random and cause you to have atypical responses. Emma Shirer was a six-year-old girl living

And then, one day, the message breaks through to our rational, verbal mind: This friend is not a friend. I am not taking my child back to that carer. This job is not for me.

in London during the Blitz. Emma had been forbidden, for as long as she could remember, from ever flushing the toilet herself, because she was too short to reach the chain without standing on the toilet seat. She thought this was unfair and embarrassing and, one night, she pulled it anyway. At that very moment, a German V-2 missile hit the house next door. The whole wall of her house disappeared and she was left gazing at open sky – still holding the chain! I met Emma when she was in her seventies; she told me she had trouble flushing toilets, or in fact doing anything slightly disobedient, for years afterwards.

Sometimes a person we meet will 'trigger' us because we have some prior experience (often called baggage) with someone similar in the past. We have to carefully check this out, because it might be true, or it might not. I automatically tend to like and trust people with a Scottish accent, because a young Scots youth worker named Jean Grigor helped me through a tough period in my teens. Fans of *Eleanor Oliphant is Completely Fine* will know that Scots people can be very kind, but it's not a universal trait of that country!

The recently identified phenomenon of 'unconscious bias' (where, without even knowing it, we assume things about people, good or bad, based on race, gender, religion, etc.) is a very good example of this baggage. It's clearly really important to shine a light onto our unconscious responses to race, gender, class, and zillions of other 'categories' we might put people in.

Many years ago, I treated Vietnam veterans who, because of the intensity and terror of that war (where you never knew who was your enemy), became terribly and understandably hypervigilant and alarmed around all Asian people. These men needed to get to know Vietnamese refugees as friends, or to return to Vietnam in peacetime to detune their memories from these false associations. Their amygdala, the place where terror occurs in the brain, had to relearn that you could be safe, happy and have fun with people with Asian features, and around the sights, smells and sounds of that country. Working out 'Is this real, or is it baggage?' is important for everyone. But you should never override your alarm system without first checking it out. We function best when we enter a kind of dialogue with our supersense, interrogating it to find what is at the bottom of those feelings. *It always has something to tell us*, and occasionally it will be life-changing.

As you learn in these pages to listen more closely to your body's signals, you will delight in how instantaneous, helpful and specific its messages are. Stopping to tune in to your supersense will require you to slow down a little, but you will avoid many time-wasting mistakes. If you think back through your life, almost all your 'accidents' or 'stuff ups' will have been accompanied by early warning signals that you rushed right past. You ignored your supersense and paid a hefty price. It's as true for the really big decisions, too: what degrees to study, what kind of job you work in, where you choose to live and who you choose to trust or be intimate with. For that reason, going slowly will actually save time, by preventing many wrong turns. And it will make life richer – slow food, slow school, slow love-making, slow holidays and slow living can lead to surprisingly exciting times, because you will be sensing and discerning what is really the best way to move through your life. In short, supersense is a sleeping powerhouse of life-guidance. It can be used every waking second, and in the coming chapters we will teach you how.

To Sum Up

In a nutshell, our ancestors bequeathed us some wonderful equipment. And at the heart of this is our supersense, which reads everything and puts it all together. But the modern world has made us stupid; we have not been raised or educated in how to read our own gauges, or listen to our own micro-cues. It's likely that an eight-year-old hunter-gatherer child a quarter of a million years ago was far more functional, capable and smart than you or I.

Getting that equipment to work is what real psychotherapy is about. My patient Andie's recovery involved her activating resources from every level of her being – her heart, her mind and her sense of connection to the universe. There were many emotions tangled up inside her. Not just from the car-park experience, but the whole of her childhood conditioning. She had to re-examine her thinking about the world she lived in. And she would emerge, not just 'put back together', not just 'normal' again (what a dreary idea), but as an even more distinctive individual, with a heightened sense of aliveness, a feeling of purpose and concern for fellow human beings. More spiritual, but in an earthy and full-throated sense. Everyone around her could see the change. She wasn't merely cured, she had gone from being simply a good person to a rather amazing one.

Everything that happens in our lives, even horror and tragedy, can be used to take us higher, and make us more free, wise and resourceful. We don't need to have a terrifying experience, though, to be fully alive. Little babies start out that way. We can learn to keep those qualities in our children, to nurture them so they stay wild and free. And we can reawaken that aliveness in ourselves. That's what we are going to explore in the chapters to come.

SUPERSENSE REFLECTION EXERCISE ONE

Looking back over your life, you will have sometimes experienced a misgiving, or just a niggle about some decision or situation you faced.

Choose one example, and give it a brief description, such as . . .

'That person I met in . . .'

'That decision I made about . . .'

'That time as a child when . . .'

Now, if you are comfortable to do so, conjure up that memory more vividly in your mind. As you do that, notice if you experience any actual body signals or responses now. Can you describe the body sensation in words – where it is and its quality or nature? E.g. a kind of clench in my stomach . . . a tight band round my forehead . . . my heart feels kind of fluttering . . . Usually one distinct place will register clearly.

Take a minute or so to just feel that, and as you pay attention to it, notice what it does, how it moves or changes. Finally, blink and look around you a bit, feel your feet on the ground and breathe in and out slowly to let the memory go. Notice that, yes, I have these 'warning lights' that go off in my body. Perhaps I can notice them more? They are helpful in living my life.

SUPERSENSE REFLECTION EXERCISE TWO

Think of a challenge or situation that is in your life right now. Some current issue, large or small – work, home or personal – that is facing you or occupying you. As you think of it, what body sensations do you notice? Where are they located – shoulders, neck, belly, face, chest? Now find a word that best describes them: tightness, heat, fluttering, tension, heaviness, wrenching, emptiness or a hole. There are thousands of words.

Just pay attention to that place, and notice if, when you name it, it changes or stays the same, or grows stronger. Later in the book, we will be helping you to shift these sensations while learning what it is they are trying to say. Take an attitude right now that this is your wise, wild-animal side letting you know something, trying to get a message to you. Send friendly thoughts to this part of yourself – you are going to become great friends, and it will be a very helpful ally for living your life.

2

Living in the Mansion

In almost every career or job today, you will find yourself sent on professional development courses from time to time. They tend to be mind-numbing affairs that have you chewing your briefcase by morning tea. I know this because, some years ago, people began to contact me and ask if I could speak to their team. The team might be midwives, teachers, funeral directors or senior police. 'Why do you want me?' I would ask, and I could hear the conspiratorial smile, even over the phone. 'Because,' they explained, 'we've heard you don't put people to sleep.'

In those days, I had mouths to feed and welcomed this employment. But I had no idea about the work of funeral directors or midwives. What could I teach them that would help in such demanding and specialized jobs? The answer wasn't hard to find – it was 'being human'. People skills – understanding oneself and others – are as vital a tool to a country police officer as to a member of a royal family or an anesthetist.

These were smart people, often far smarter than me, so I

always came from a position of respecting their life experience. Standing in front of the audience, when the day came, after the due introductions, I would begin by asking them to answer a deceptively simple question: 'What is a human being?' People would look puzzled for a moment or two, and then start scribbling. After a couple of minutes, I would ask them to call out what they had written.

Some people's answers were concrete and simple: a human being is an animal, a two-legged mammal, or something along those lines. Others in the audience said that we are a social being. The more idealistic in the room added that we have huge potential and that we grow and learn. Some pointed out that we have emotions and values, and dreams. Some ventured into spiritual domains – that we are created by or are the children of God, or, in secular language, that we are a mix of mind, body and spirit.

This is not a trivial exercise, because our model of what a human being is will powerfully shape both the person we are and how we treat others. The depressed person will have a depressing idea of what a human being is, and the kindly person will have a kindly view. The angry, resentful person will have a pretty crappy view. You'll notice immediately that something important is going on here. If you don't think much of human beings, then *deep down you don't think much of yourself either*. It's not hard to see how this can be self-reinforcing and really get out of hand. I am repeating myself here because I don't want you to miss this: what you think a human being is, is *probably the most important thing about you*, because it determines how you treat everyone you ever meet, and how you treat yourself. So you need to be absolutely sure you haven't got a wrong-headed idea about such an important fact.

I have had many patients who as children or teenagers were told by their parents, with great force and repetition, that they were 'a piece of shit', or something along those lines. Few people come out of that kind of childhood without some serious scars. But even for a child coming from a kind and loving family, there are still the messages of the larger world to contend with. The culture around us essentially tells us we are just one big appetite, or one big ego. If we fall for this – and few can be completely immune to it – then we will never be happy. If we are to live a full life then it's critical that we have the best and most complete view of what a human being is, what we ourselves are. The whole point of this book is to dramatically expand your view of what makes up a human being, what makes up *you*.

The people in my training seminars always, without prompting, arrive at a conclusion that human beings have *multiple dimensions,* that there are layers or levels to what we are. And this is definitely true from a neuroscience viewpoint; our brain's structure, and therefore our consciousness – the way our brain works – is layered. Old, primitive, reptilian structures lie underneath, while more mammalian (warm-blooded and warm-hearted) layers are on top of those, and then the truly human layers of insight and empathy are on the very outermost surface. It matches our evolution – lizards don't cuddle or nurture their babies, mammals do. But hedgehogs and badgers don't worry about finding a good school for their offspring!

We Have Layers – So What?

You might be thinking, Well, yes, I sort of knew that – I am a multidimensional being, sure. I have a thinking part, an emotional part, and so on. But how does that help? The answer is that, while we might pay lip service to this idea, in reality most people today ignore or neglect most of their levels. The average person is trapped in a tiny corner of their mind, usually a stale and scratchy bubble of self-talk that goes round and round, while all the time a wonderful richness of aliveness and connection lies unused all around them.

Our culture has wiped out whole areas of consciousness that would have been available to someone living fifty thousand years ago, and, in some surviving cultures, still is. What we pay attention to and what we ignore is strongly conditioned as we grow up, and usually our parents did not attend to or nurture many aspects of our awareness, if they even knew about them. For example, some families simply never have conversations about emotions. Those topics were entirely absent from my 1950s childhood. My wife, Shaaron, had a much tougher childhood, where the kids mostly made their own meals and cleaned up the house, as their parents were so busy working to survive. She cannot remember a single instance of her parents asking how she was, or how her day had been. But even in very normal families today, most of what is happening inside a child is not enquired into. Teenagers, too, have depths of questioning and hungers of a spiritual kind that we never touch on. Without having their inner world drawn out, affirmed and given a language to express itself, young people become like a tiger raised in a cage, huge energies untapped, huge potentials buried. The interior worlds of most people today are shrivelled and unrealized.

Of course, some people fare better than others. In my *Raising Girls* book and talks, I tell the story of a teenage girl, Genevieve, whose boyfriend is starting to pressure her to have sex. She is deeply confused and asks her mother what she should do. Her mother tells her something very wise. She says, 'Well, honey, usually somewhere deep down, your body knows what's right for you.' And instantly, the daughter knows. She feels loving towards this boy, but she does not feel ready to have sex with him. It's crystal clear. When I describe this to my audiences, you can hear a sigh of recognition ripple across the auditorium.

But most people are not raised with awareness of their multiple layers (the physical is only one of many). Think of how many times in life you have done something or chosen something when large parts of you were screaming 'No!!' Or you've not done something when large parts of you were urging 'Yes!!' And so we end up living in a very unnatural and odd

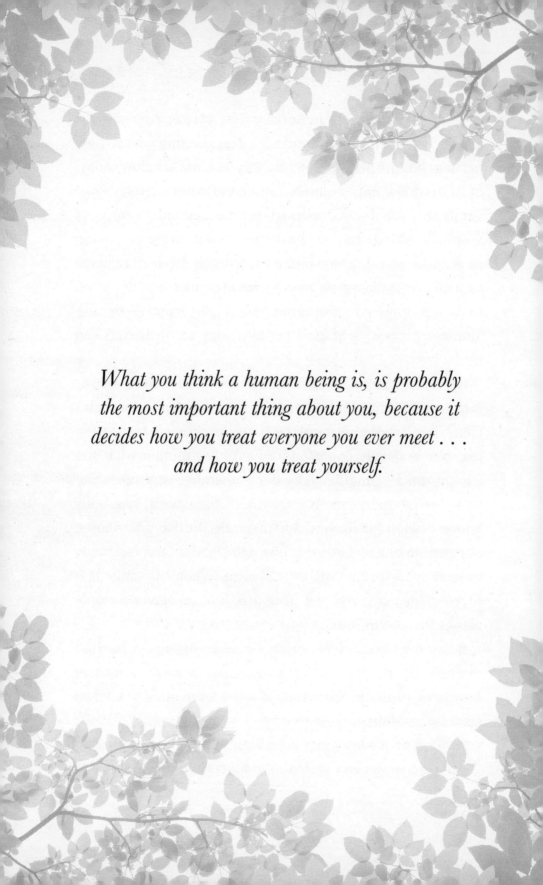

What you think a human being is, is probably the most important thing about you, because it decides how you treat everyone you ever meet . . . and how you treat yourself.

way, obedient and conforming, blotting out huge areas of our consciousness. Powerful tools for living go quite unused.

There is a deeper problem here as well. If we ignore a part of us – our feelings, our body, our values, our sexuality or our spirituality – that part does not just lie quiescent. It continues to exert a force on us, but just without our knowing it! It is like an inner mutiny, which we can't read or integrate. And since some of those layers are very powerful, we can end up absolutely torn in pieces, deeply conflicted and confused. And we just don't add up as a human being. Our life won't make sense.

When we don't access all areas of our own layered mind, our lives lose their integrity. Others experience us as incongruous, untrustworthy. We become sleepwalkers in our own lives. And losing our power in this way, we become easily enslaved.[1] The hyper capitalist life – rushing, stressing, consuming – takes a terrible toll on families, which we just assume is normal. And if it's normal, then there must be something wrong with us – and our family – that we can't keep up. Just as women in the 1950s thought there must be something wrong with them when they weren't fulfilled in aprons, cooking scones, contemporary men and women feel inadequate that they can't sustain the lonely, competitive harshness of twenty-first-century life. Our children, too, are growing up in a world that's increasingly nasty, aggressive and punishing of everyone who does not meet impossible standards in things that really don't matter at all – such as fashion, body shape, possessions.

So many really terrible problems that readers will recognise – divorce, anxiety and stress in children, rebellion and self-harm in teenagers – are the direct consequence of this. People who are integrated and in touch with their power do not put up with the way of life that is handed out to them, they look for something better. They start marching to a different drum. These are the people who change the world. Our hope lies in more and more of us doing just that.

When we learn to incorporate and use all the layers of our humanness, amazing things can happen, we find our own rhythm and our own power. So now it's time to set out for you what those levels and layers are, and how to move about in them. It's time to tell you about the Four-Storey Mansion.

The Four Storeys of Your Human House

Our minds are complex things, and so, to manage them, we need simple and workable tools – handles we can grab hold of. I struggled for many years to find a language or way to bring the findings of neuroscience, on the one hand, and the methods of psychotherapy, on the other, into a single system that could be used by anyone, in any situation. A model or map simple enough that you could explain it to a little child, and flexible enough that, on a bad day or in a sudden emergency, you could call on it and it would offer immediate help. And finally, some deep-down part of my brain provided it for me – the metaphor of the Four-Storey Mansion.

I loved this idea from the outset, and I both use it and teach it all the time. Probably like you, I have had serious things to deal with in my life, and this model has carried me through, so far. (And, living at a time of human crisis, while growing old myself, it gets more relevant by the day.)

So let's start the tour. Right now, sitting there reading this book, try this out. Notice how you are sitting, how comfortable or uncomfortable you are. (If you want to shift a little, just do that.) Keep noticing your overall physical state. What are the sensations you can feel in your belly? Your back? What expression is on your face? Are you breathing?

The foundations of who you are, the ground floor of your mansion, is a physical, mammalian body that acts and senses. It needs food, it needs sleep, it needs to move and dance and play. It needs to make love and make music. It needs to be in nature. This seems so obvious, but often people ignore or neglect those aspects of their life, and wonder that things aren't going well. Further on, we will devote a chapter to awakening and developing richer neural pathways into your physical self, and you will find this becomes a more enlivened and pleasure-bringing resource, as well as a way to process all kinds of difficulty, and to restore balance and wellbeing. For now, just be aware – the first floor is your body. It's always there, and it's always worth a visit!

Now, let's go up another floor in your multi-storey house. Next up, arising out of your body but with a floor of its own, we have an emotional level, a 'heart', full of feelings. Feelings arise out of your body but are different from mere sensations. For example, you can be hungry and pleased, as you are on a diet or a health fast, and it's going well. Or you can be hungry and furious, because you walked away from your things at the beach and seagulls ate your lunch. Or you can be hungry and scared, because you are on a hike and lost, and the food is getting low. Same sensation, different meaning.

Emotions are a more distinct and intense level than mere sensation. They mean something, something important to figure out. Emotions – fear, anger, sadness and joy – tell you the deep truth about something, usually right here and now. They also energize you in a certain way that will help you get through a situation. Emotions are a kind of intelligence, and they are especially important for relating to others. We'll give you a world-class guide to emotions in The Second Floor chapter, so you can have your feelings work for you instead of the other way around.

GUT FEELINGS AND EMOTIONS CAN CLASH

It's important to be clear that your supersense is not the same thing as your emotions. It's deeper than your emotions, further down, if you like, and more inclusive and holistic. Here is an example . . .

Roisin is thirty-two and has been in a relationship with Iain for three years. He is kind, comfortable to be around, she trusts him. But she is troubled by a recurring thought that he is not the right man for her. She finds him, in a word, dull. Lately, these feelings have been getting stronger. Something inside her just goes 'Erk' when she thinks about spending the rest of her life with him. Her gut says, in effect: 'You need someone with more fire and purpose.' But her emotions, whenever this thought comes up, are of fear, of losing the relationship and being alone. So her feelings say, 'Stay', but her supersense whispers, 'You will never be happy with this man.' This message seems to come from somewhere deeper and wiser, but quieter, than just emotions.

When we have these competing messages inside us, it's not a matter of one being right and the other wrong, more of a process that needs to be attended to and allowed to unfold. She continues to listen to her insides, and to be honest and open with her partner, to see how things go.

After some time, Roisin and Iain do separate, and they do it kindly and without recrimination. In the months that follow, Roisin feels more and more clear that the relationship wasn't right for her, and she is happier, and more authentic and strong being on her own again. It's challenging to be alone, and she still hopes one day to be in a relationship that is a better fit. But it will have to be right. Interestingly, after they part, Iain leaves his job and he too sets off on some adventures towards living a larger life. (Family therapists reading this will smile, knowing that no human being is 'dull' but we can all get caught in a system where we are not our full selves.)

The main message here is – if Roisin had 'listened to her emotions' alone, she would have stayed stuck. Her supersense had a different message. It took a while to find, but it made all the difference. No part of our mansion has the whole picture, but if we consult on all levels, things are more likely to go well.

Now, let's go up another storey, up into your head. Here, on the third floor, planted on top of your body and your emotions, you have a brain that thinks (though not always very well). This is your prefrontal cortex, your executive and analytical brain. Most people, when they think of themselves, think of their thoughts. I think therefore I am. But nothing could be further from the truth! We do urgently need to think better, and I hope this book will give you some powerful tools to sharpen and grow this capacity. Thinking is the way we make sense of our lives, and also how we communicate with others around us – putting things into words and sending them out there. Listening and changing in response to the thoughts of others helps us to relate well, and also to update or challenge our own perspective. Words are a bridge to the rest of the human race. The third floor of our mansion is a lively and sparky kind of place. But a major message, here: this is not remotely the totality of you. It's just a tool, and the real you is so much more than your thinking. Rather like in a big organization, the CEO matters, but only if everyone in the place participates fully and works together. As your brain learns to respect all your other parts, then things can really begin to hum.

Up on the Roof

Now, having explored the three storeys of the house, many people would say, 'That's it, then. Body, emotion, thought: that's the whole human package.' But it's not – there's more! Instead of thinking down into yourself, think outwards now, to the world around you – people, things, and beyond, to the sky and the stars. Then think of the endless sweep of time, past and future, and the chain of lives that have come before you and will go on after you. From this perspective, it's not hard to realize that you are a very small event in a very big universe.

But, in realizing this, as we all sooner or later do, people often make two big mistakes. The first is they feel inconsequential. And second, they think that they are alone in a big uncaring world. It's not far from this to becoming very depressed. Suicide, that most tragic and wasteful of endings, is when it all boils down – death from loneliness. In most modern countries, suicide is an immense problem, killing thousands of people each year. Many other lesser problems, too – greed, addiction, anxiety, selfishness – are also the result of this mistaken way of thinking about yourself.

So, let me lay it on the line for you, right here and now: you are not separate or inconsequential. You are as much a part of everything as a leaf is a part of a tree, or a raindrop the ocean. Without the leaves, there is no tree. Without the raindrops, there is no ocean. So it's very important, if we are to be realistic and rational in our lives, that we take this into account. We are part of something big, going somewhere big, and our lives will thrive – and matter – if we are tuned in to this. Life is a dance, a party waiting for us to join in, and it's also a project needing our contribution – the project of human thriving. This book will give you ways not just to intellectually grasp this (for that is a meagre consolation), but to actually experience a felt sense of dissolving into the exuberance that is the natural world, and the brotherhood and sisterhood that is humanity, so you don't ever need to feel on your own. As the great religious traditions have love at their core – so often buried, but still shining through – you too are loved.

The fourth floor of our mansion – where we connect to everything – is the home of our spirituality. The place where – either by luck or grace, or by hard work – you have a sense that you are connected to all around you, to the sacred unity of everything. This is not a matter of faith, but simply a direct sense of fellowship and belonging in the world, with which we are born, and which we can hopefully continue to know as our life unfolds.

There is a reason why spirituality is the *top* floor; this sense is essential to making our body–mind systems work as they should. Just as your mobile phone is pretty limited without being linked to the network, your life makes no sense except when it's tuned in to the wider life around you.

This topmost floor is not like the others. It's a rooftop garden, open to the sky. Spirituality is notoriously difficult to express in words, because words are designed to address small, discrete things – spoon, dog, nostrils – and not huge mysteries. But can you remember ever as a child just feeling wonderful? Completely and fully free and alive? I can recall times as a little boy, running on a windy beach, seagulls wheeling above, waves crashing, clouds towering out over the ocean, feeling absolutely, totally free and somehow part of it all. Do you remember ever feeling that way? Totally safe, without boundaries or self-consciousness of any kind? Where was that? How old were you?

Spirituality is about regaining that sense of freedom and unity, and all that flows out of that. Compassion. Peace. Creativity. A dissolving of the troublesomeness of having an ego to defend. An easy harmony with life. And from that, a wish to end suffering, to become a steward of the human and natural world – because you are joined to it. And who would not care for a part of themselves?

There are many practices and ways of thinking, which you will discover in these pages, to get to that place. You can be planted solidly on the roof of your house, as you gaze out from it, and gradually realize that you don't even need the house at all. You can live without fear and do the most extraordinary things. It will take a whole book to unfold this idea, but now we've taken the first step. The journey has begun.

Lining Up Your Floors

There is one more thing, the most important thing, which we saved until last. When you begin to live on all four floors of your mansion, something will very quickly become evident. For almost all of us, the floors will sometimes, perhaps often, be at odds with each other. Our feelings will not match our actions. Our body will want something that our brain says it can't have. Our brain won't listen to our soul. Your life, in other words, won't stack up. So this next piece of information is critical. Listen closely . . .

As the final step in the day that I spend with midwives, funeral directors, surgeons or soldiers, learning about the Four-Storey Mansion, I ask them to do something challenging. I ask them to sit with two or three other people and discuss 'How does your life stack up?' The invariable result is that discussions begin that are almost impossible to shut down. I can't get them to stop. People huddle intensely; faces are animated; in parts of the room, people are crying and others comforting them. The question is simply the most profound one you can ask.

Noticing the non-alignment of your life – even if it makes you weep with despair – is part of the healing. You don't have to consciously know what to do, yet. That will emerge. A human being, like any living creature, naturally seeks unity in all its parts.

And the universe does too. We can help this by just bringing our attention to where we might have conflict or discomfort. Then our system will find a way to heal that.

All we have to do is notice. And keep breathing. And going on with our lives, bravely keeping all four floors occupied, with the lights on. Our miraculous body–mind system will begin to tell us what to do, and how to do it. We will put ourselves together, however long it takes. And that will make all the difference.

LIVING IN THE MANSION
REFLECTION EXERCISES ONE TO SEVEN

1. Are you aware of having different levels to your consciousness? Before reading this book, was that something you normally and actively tuned in to during your day-to-day life?

2. A key skill we will be learning in the book is 'mobility' up and down inside your mansion, rather like going up and down in a lift. Are you able to go down into your body easily and notice sensations? (To begin with, just ordinary things – physical comfort, tight muscles, temperature, relaxation?)

3. Are you in touch with emotions, generally, when you have them?

4. Does it come easily to you to calm down and think clearly, reason things out?

5. Do you have a sense of spirituality, of being safe and at home in the universe? Of being part of the larger whole of nature, including other people? Just a little, or a lot? Or is that an alien concept to you?

6. In short, which levels – body, emotion, intellect and spirit – do you occupy, and which do you mostly not notice?

7. Most importantly, is there a level that you tend to get stuck in? Does that cause you trouble in living your life?

If you haven't been aware of your levels, you are going to have a lot of fun and freedom through exploring them, and your life will be significantly easier as you do. Allow yourself, on the second floor, to feel some excitement. Breathe and make some room for that!

3

THE FIRST FLOOR

Your Body

I am sitting opposite a client who has serious post-traumatic stress. He has served in some of the worst war zones in the world, and so what he is experiencing is very understandable. But the help he has received to date has not been adequate. He has been in and out of hospital, has been seriously suicidal multiple times, and his family has been badly affected by the intense emotions that still sweep through him.

Right now, he is talking very intensely about his situation, but there is something more important that is drawing my attention. It's the way he is holding his body: he is perched on the edge of his chair, as if getting ready to run away. He holds his fists tight. His breath is shallow and fast. As soon as I can, I gently ask if I may interrupt him. I ask him how his body is feeling, what sensations are happening inside him. He looks suddenly bewildered, as if it's completely off topic. I quietly say, 'Would you just notice if you are comfortable in the chair?' He tentatively sits back, and the big comfy chair supports him. I ask him if he could take a pause from talking, just for a few seconds, and breathe. He smiles, and some colour comes into

For our clients to be able to heal, we therapists have to care for them with an intensity (of focus and resolve — of love, really) that matches the intensity with which they were harmed.

his face. He is an intelligent man, and he isn't slow to work things out. He smiles because he recognizes in a flash that, in the way he was sitting, breathing and speaking, he was being scared in a place that was actually very, very safe. His mind had been out of his body and caught in the past. From this starting point, he is open to realizing that even something as complex as PTSD (post-traumatic stress disorder) is still at heart a physical problem, and when he pays attention to his body, he can improve things in small ways that will add up to a large change in time.

Part of the failed help that this man and thousands of others with PTSD received has been the over-reliance on CBT (cognitive behavioural therapy) and the idea that thought can control feeling. Of course it is important to confront faulty thinking, but it is rarely enough, because our brains are wired in largely the opposite direction. Emotions so very often are what is driving thought. And by the same token, it is important to also intervene at the level of body awareness and get behind the feelings, to the supersense where they begin. To let the body resolve things one layer at a time, working with the Four-Storey Mansion from the ground up. By doing this, the therapist creates a direct experience of being in a safe place, both actually and relationally. For our clients to be able to heal, we therapists have to care for them with an intensity (of focus and resolve – of love, really) that matches the intensity with which they were harmed.

In every stage of his recovery, his body will serve as an ally. Returning to his inner sensations, allowing them to settle and clarify, and adding some physical exercise like walking or swimming, yoga or tai chi, will ground him in the here and now. His body will become a reliable way to create a temporary haven. We will then, and only then, be able to work with the torrent of unexpressed emotions, with the tangled patterns of thought, and with questions of meaning and spirit, which we need to do to create lasting change and growth out of the terrible place he is in. But using his supersense to come back to his body will always be the safe anchor we return to. Breathe. Open your eyes. Feel your feet supported by the ground. Be here now.

My client is not unique in ignoring his body and, as a result, getting hopelessly caught up in memories and fears. In fact, most people have this problem to some degree. No culture in history has ignored the body as much as ours. The modern world of planes, cars and supermarkets was built by a certain kind of man and woman. The Calvinist founders of capitalism itself came from a European Protestant tradition of cold and austere repression of pleasure, built over a strong foundation of self-flagellating Catholic guilt, often marinated in several other ethnicities with problems of their own. Northern Europeans were never the singing-and-dancing-est culture in the world. Whenever we arrived in other places in the world (usually to colonize and make other people miserable), the locals were greatly struck by how uptight and generally messed up we were.

Having this kind of background and regarding it as normal – being cut off from body, from emotion and from spirituality, all but abandoning three whole floors of our Four-Storey Mansion – means that, when the inevitable traumas of life come along, we are very ill-equipped to process them. The problem is not the trauma, but the lack of ability to let our natural healing systems do their job.

How We Lost Touch with Our Bodies

It wasn't my client's fault that he had grown up from childhood with an inability to feel. It was the legacy of generations of messed-upness. Our great grandparents' whole lives were built on emotional repression. 'Sit still, be quiet, stop your snivelling. Toughen up. Off to boarding school at six, I survived, it made a man of me.' Adulthood was just more of the same. Men back then were systematically shaped to be the cannon fodder of empire. Women were conditioned for lives of drudgery and sexual frustration. It involved massive suppression of one's true feelings. All that suppression is hard work, shutting your body's inner signals down, holding muscles tight. A stiff upper lip wasn't just a turn of phrase, it was advice given to soldiers to get through the profound grief of seeing their friends blown to bits. Straighten your back, jut your jaw. Push on. Think of England.

HOW A 'NIGHTMARE CENTURY' WAS WRITTEN IN OUR BODIES

We've come to assume that Westerners – especially the English – were always buttoned-down walking time bombs of emotional repression. But really that is very much a product of recent history. And it is reflected most intensely in our bodies. The tension of emotional suppression hurts so much you will do almost anything to take it away. That physical pain is probably the reason for our astonishing dependence in the West on alcohol. The *Mad Men* post-war generation of the 1950s and '60s were awash with booze. For working-class Englishmen, an hour or more in the pub, getting plastered, was the routine every night after work. (Women drank alone at home, in quantities that would shock us today.) By the 1960s, the most prescribed drug in the Western world was valium, a muscle relaxant given as a tranquillizer. These self-medicating strategies numbed the problem, but did nothing to solve it.

Around the time of the Vietnam War, with its body counts on the evening news like a grotesque sports score, and sons and brothers coming home in zippered bags, a seismic cultural shift began. It started on the American West Coast, rebounded off swinging London, tripped off to Rishikesh and then back to Woodstock, and pretty much swept the world. Young people dared to question the motives of their politicians, and, in a university called Kent State, they were proven right. Trust in authority, which had prevailed in a way we can barely credit today, disintegrated. Parenting author and paediatrician Benjamin Spock was blamed for this new generation's questioning of authority, but only after he started supporting the anti-war movement and brought Middle America with him. Perhaps more affectionate parenting by the post-war generation did play a part. This was not a mere change in clothing or hair fashions, it challenged the basis of an entire civilization built on conformity and fear. And it was still going fifty years later, from Pussy Riot in Russia to the blood-stained cobblestones of Tiananmen Square. To Greta Thunberg and the School Strike for Climate. To Black Lives Matter. In the 1960s and '70s, a significant cohort of human beings got in touch with their hearts and values and their love and connection with the natural world, and the genie was out of the bottle. Out of that came a new wave of feminism, environmentalism, gay rights, indigenous rights and animal liberation. We recognized that this was a battle of the forces of life versus the forces of death. The climate emergency may be its ultimate fight, but we've come a long way, and there is much reason to hope.

In From the Cold

Today, we trust and enjoy our bodies more. We take joy in children laughing and playing and making noise (up to a point). We are happy to see our teenagers surf or dance, make music or art, or take a year or two to travel the world. Sexual happiness is encouraged and expected (in fact, it's kind of mandatory, though that's another story). Pleasure is okay at last. Nature is being conceived as our home, not as something to be conquered and mined into oblivion. And somehow, central to all of this, emotionally we have much more scope. We allow ourselves to cry – even men, sometimes.

But there is a long way to go yet. Compared with the flexibility and sensitivity of a little child, adults are still numb and stiff, and new pressures and conformities are thrust onto us by social media and competitive consumerism. We remain drastically out of touch with our inner lives. It takes more than just a generation or two to break the mould of centuries. But break it we must, if we are to return to the garden that life was intended to be, to even basic mental health and wellbeing, let alone a sustainable Earth shared by balanced human beings. It's our own selves that we have to explore and liberate. In this book, we will help you travel that country. And if you are a parent, we will also help you to ensure that your kids need never leave it in the first place.

Coming Back to Your Body

In the rest of this chapter, we will teach you how to activate the parts of your brain that sense, interpret and direct your body. This process is quite remarkable because, down there, just south of your neck, there is a whole symphony orchestra playing, and the music is always changing. Your body is calling out to you, wanting to help you live your life. It's a wise wild creature that wants to be your friend.

Your mind and body are built for health and happiness, but they need one thing from you in order to work properly – your attention. It's your attention that moves through the four storeys of your house, that listens to your supersense. Picture a small figure with a torch, going about turning lights on! As you read this book, you will experience, hundreds of times, your attention moving about with greater and greater awareness and choice. As you shine the light of your own awareness into your own insides, just casually and naturally, at odd times during your day, you will start to find everything improves – as basic as digestion or posture, as profound as peace and serenity and life-changing insights. That little dancing laser beam is your freedom. You can point yourself in any direction you choose!

Getting Started

We'll start straight away – here is something to try. Right now, without putting down the book or device you are reading, just elevate your little finger on your right hand (like an English person taking tea). Okay. Now, do it a few times, and as you do, notice *any other movements or sensations elsewhere in your body.* I'll wait while you do it! You may feel some slight shifts in your hand, of course, but what about your other hand?

Your feet? Your trunk? At first, you might feel nothing at all. Really pay attention and scan around your body. What else changes, ever so slightly? If you have trouble, try something a little larger. Lift your whole right arm in the air. Where else can you feel sensation, a slight tightening of a muscle, a small movement?

What we know, from electrically measuring muscle potentials, is that, when you move even your little finger, every other muscle in your body adjusts slightly. Even the toes on your left foot shift just a little to counterbalance the tiny change of weight in your hand, or what it expects might come next. Muscle movements begin so subtly that, even when watching a tennis match or a dance contest, parts of your body rehearse the movements you are seeing.

We are often completely unaware of how we move. When you raise your arm, it's not your arm that actually creates that movement. Try it again and see. Your arm is moved by your shoulders and the muscles in your back. Any movement in your body involves all of the rest of your body.

You are probably sitting right now, so try this: don't do anything, don't move at all, but imagine getting up from your chair. Rehearse that movement in your mind. Small changes will immediately happen in your neck, back and legs as they get ready for the whole-body requirement that such a move would have. If you don't feel these things, don't worry; by the end of this book you will have loosened up.

Now, fascinating as this is, it's not where we are going here (and I am indebted for this to Moshe Feldenkrais, the Israeli

physicist and judo champion, whose exercise and body awareness system has changed the lives of thousands of people).
Where this matters most is to alert you to how much is
happening inside you, in every second of your life.

Muscles are only the most superficial level of this. Organs,
too, move and change, often in response to things happening
around us. Our stomach clenches. Our mouth goes dry. The
changes may be fleeting, or more major and long-lasting.
Norwegian researchers found that, in a bereavement situation
– the loss of a loved husband or wife, or a child – the shape of
our heart itself changes. It tightens across the top half of the
organ, and it stays that way for as long as a year. What is going
on here? Are we literally broken-hearted? Most likely it's a kind
of shutdown, a slowing, but is it a sign of healthy grief, or
repressed grief – of grief gone wrong? After all, people in the
West are not big on expressing grief, compared with many parts
of the world. If we could sob, wrack and keen, surrounded by
family and friends all doing the same, as might happen in some
cultures, would this heart-clenching still happen? All we know
for sure is that the body remembers. It's not inconsequential
– a bereaved person is many times more likely to die in the first
year after a loss like this, from totally natural causes. [2,3] It's
especially so in the first days and weeks.

Our organs are full of nerve endings – especially our digestive tract and stomach – and the reason for this is unclear, but
there is bound to be one. It is almost certainly behind the
expression that occurs in many languages: gut feelings. When
we have powerful experiences, we describe them as *moving*;

we experience almost all the emotions as great heaving tides or shifts in our bodies. It can be literally overwhelming, bringing us to our knees, unable to function until that emotion is properly discharged and has done its job.

We can even like and enjoy this. The ending of a great movie or book, or a piece of music, can sweep us with emotion, and great effort and skill goes into making that happen. Emotion is the reason why we go to the movies, read novels or attend music concerts. We remember for years afterwards that intense, soaring feeling as the music swells and credits start to roll. They made it to safety. She really did love him. The hobbits survived and were praised by all in Middle Earth.

And unless we are lacking a heartbeat, we have those moments in our own lives as well. And it's in our body that they register. Falling in love, feeling desire, worrying about our kids, adoring our grandchildren – all these are visceral.

Long ago, my wife and I lived on a large sheep property beneath Tasmania's Great Western Tiers. We would often walk out in the fields in the early morning. On seeing us suddenly arrive in their midst, the newly wakened sheep would, en masse, pee copiously onto the grass before scampering away. Hundreds of sheep urinating at once is a hilarious sight, a Niagara Falls experience! In his bestselling book *Wolf Totem*, Chinese writer Jiang Rong describes the Mongolian steppe wolves surprising the deer at dawn, because their full bladders prevented them running. So peeing and pooing when danger threatens has a practical reason: it lightens the load! Humans have that reaction too, if terrible danger threatens. Australian schoolboys joke about 'packing your daks', but in the wild it's a practical and useful thing. Our bodily reactions can be intense, because life itself for human beings can be extreme. Tragically, extreme stress can even bring on early labour. We were designed for hard times.

In the modern world, we can be too safe; so numbed and bored that we actually seek out the enlivening quickening of some faux danger. The murder mysteries beloved of old folks always begin with the frisson of a terrible murder. Suitably stirred up, the viewers settle in for the crossword-puzzle contentment of finding out 'whodunnit'. Younger people get their kicks in the real world: teenagers drive cars too fast or, more healthily, brave the surf or the mountain-bike trails; young couples ride roller coasters; highly trained health professionals are often drawn to extreme sports or outdoor pursuits, even though these may endanger their lives. Everyone watches the evening news; we say it's to be informed, but really it just makes us feel more alive. (It's possible we need more actual involvement with real people's needs, if we seek distress and drama as entertainment.) But the point is, we are physical, in a body, and that body responds. To everything.

This is our first and most basic lesson – since it is probably not how you have thought or operated, up until today. Your body has a life all of its own. It is doing its job beautifully all the time. It provides motivation, for good or for ill, and will affect you whether you acknowledge it or not. It gives you vital clues. It steers you towards health and aliveness. Your life can go more smoothly if you listen to its voice, not just when it is screaming at you, but quietly and often as you go through your day.

YOUR BODY IS ALSO YOUR MIND – THE TECHNIQUE OF FOCUSING

Modern psychology didn't start with rats in mazes, or people on couches talking about their mothers, but with a man called Carl Rogers. Rogers had a superb mind but also a warm heart, and he refused to believe that those two things should be separated. He took things out of the chilly hands of the men in white coats and founded what we now call Humanistic Psychology. Rogers and a handful of his colleagues basically invented the modern idea of counselling.

Rogers knew something fundamental to human wellbeing – that, to come through the worst times in life, we all need someone who really listens deeply to us, and does not interrupt with their own agenda. If you have ever been well cared for by a counsellor or had a doctor who gave you time and their full attention, you have Rogers to thank.

But working alongside Carl Rogers was a man who took things further still, and whose work is just beginning to be fully acknowledged. Eugene Gendlin was, in my view and that of many who knew him, a genius. He is really the grandfather of this book in your hands right now.

Gendlin and Rogers found that some people, right from the get-go, responded very well to counselling, and some just did not. So they studied videotapes minutely to find out what the difference was. Those who grew, healed and flew ahead did something very distinct. When the counsellor asked something, they did not glibly rattle off some words, they did something different – they paused, then *went inside themselves* to find the answer . . .

'Are you angry with your husband?' Pause, reflects. 'No, well, I am, but there is more this feeling of despair, like, *can he even change?* I feel a bit hopeless, and sad for him too . . .'

In every instance where a client in counselling was on the edge of growth or new insight, there was a point where they had to search inside themselves for what was true. They did not know what their true feelings were, and that was the key to unlocking internal change. The answer at first seemed fuzzy, but, with some more focus, it would suddenly clarify. The client struggled for words, perhaps made a few false guesses, rejected those, and then – *bang* – there it was. They found the word or understanding that was true, and their body shifted with relief.

The client in counselling needs to feel safe, and if they feel safe, they can be honest, but *they can only be honest if they know their own hearts*. And some people go through life never doing this. My old mum was like this: she would say she was 'fine' even when she was 'spitting chips', because, in her childhood, you never ever complained or expressed annoyance, let alone anger. It wasn't the ladylike thing, or the Christian thing, or even the sane thing to do.

If you don't practise going inside yourself, pretty soon you forget you even have an inside. And that is a problem. People who do bad things to others are invariably people who cannot manage their own insides, and so they try to feel better by hurting others. Think abusive partners. Think terrorists and mass shooters. Think tyrants and drug addicts. But also many, many people who just feel lost and confused. Lack of self-awareness is the most crippling disability a human being can have.

Gendlin knew this ability to check inside was vital to well-being, and he set out to help people gain that skill. His book about the subject, simply titled *Focusing*, sold half a million copies. What Gendlin came to believe was that we have a 'second brain', a second locus of awareness, which of course is what I call supersense. For every dilemma we face in life, there is a body awareness that has captured this, and that can guide you.

How to do Focusing

To understand what I mean, just try this. Settle yourself down in your seat, then simply choose or think of a problem that you have at the moment. (Most of us have plenty we can choose from(!), but just settle on one for this exercise.) Perhaps one of your family who concerns you, or some issue in life that is proving difficult. Just hold that person or situation in your mind.

As you do this, you will almost certainly feel, somewhere in your body, a sensation that seems to go with this problem. It will be hard to describe, but it is physical – somewhere tenses or feels hollow or heats up, or squirms just a little, or there is a pang of pain. That is the place. You've found the

In every instance where a client was on the edge of new insight, there was a point where they had to search inside themselves. The answer at first seemed fuzzy, but, with more focus, it would suddenly clarify. They found the word that was true, and their body shifted with relief.

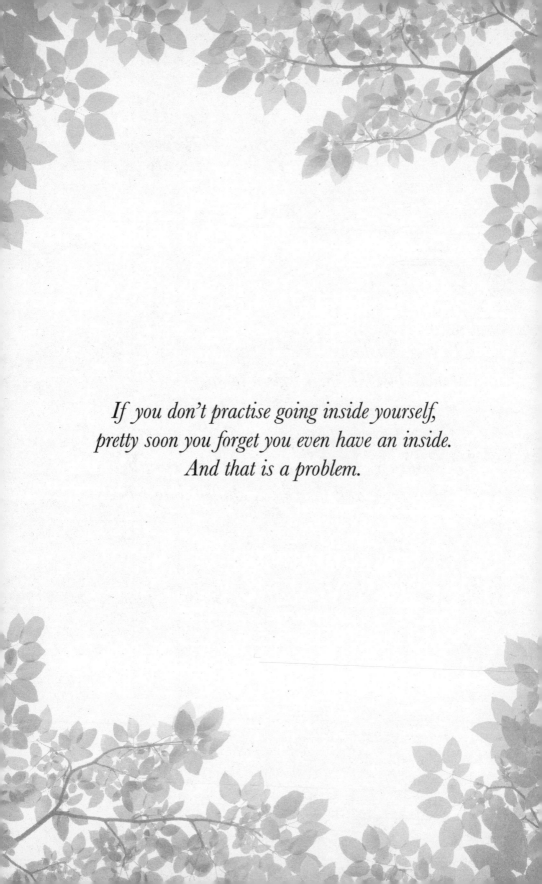

If you don't practise going inside yourself,
pretty soon you forget you even have an inside.
And that is a problem.

spot. (If you can't feel it, don't worry, for many people it can take a while to calm down enough, and then it comes, 'Oh, *that* thing'. Even a 'nothing' feeling is a feeling, so start there.) If you are still having trouble, another way is to make an opposite statement, mentally or out loud, like, 'Everything in my life is wonderful' and listen to the almost-instant squawk that comes from somewhere in your body, saying, in effect, 'Oh yeah?'

This feeling will have a quality of freshness as you pay it more attention, of something half-formed, just emerging. This is a lively part of your non-conscious brain working with your body's physiology to send a supersense message to you. Gendlin calls the sensation 'the murky edge', because what it means is just out of grasp. Like your edge in a yoga pose, where you gently stretch just a little more, this is your consciousness edge, the very boundary where you are progressing as a human being (and you thought it was just indigestion!).

Once you have found the sensation that is there right now, the next step is to 'enquire' of that place, seeing if you can name it and what it feels like – hesitation, fear, fury, frustration, loneliness, disappointment; feeling kinds of names, but very specific. It's important to give it a word that is the closest fit you can find – even just 'tight' or 'empty' or 'hunched' – and your body will in fact 'tell' you if this is the right word. This gives your logical mind a 'handle' to relate to your supersense message at this specific point in time.

It's almost like tentatively reaching out to a wild animal inside you, building a relationship to gain its trust. If you pay attention to this place in your body, it *welcomes* your noticing it. And here is the most amazing part – when you try to name it, it will 'tell' you, yes, or no, or 'keep trying, you're close'. As you put names to the sensation, it often changes, and the message changes too. For this is the nub of the thing: when you listen to your insides, they inform you how to change, where the answer might lie. And when you have really 'got' the message, even just wordlessly making space for it, it very often shifts. You feel a change in your body that is positive, releasing, enlivening, and you know that something has moved, that you are different now.

Focusing is a skill that is subtle, and it's best you read Gendlin's book, or watch some of the many YouTube talks and demonstrations. But go just a little way into this and the immense possibilities start to open up, because this is supersense made available at any time, or all the time, allowing you to really begin to use it intelligently for informing your life.

Gendlin believed (and he was a highly respected academic philosopher) that there is no difference between body and mind. That every inch of our body is mind. Nerves, hormones, muscles all talk to each other, they are a unity. Our physical body is not (as we have been taught to think), a biological machine, but is a consciousness that arose out of nature, shaped by our mother's body and the parenting we received, and all our interactions in life since. (Children's broadcaster Fred Rogers used to ask people to reflect on 'Who are the adults who loved you into existence?') Whole areas of your brain only grow if you are loved and stimulated. It isn't a metaphor. Your body *is* your mind. Our 'felt sense', our supersense, is the way we experience that, and our little orange-rind cortex that thinks in words is a vital, but only partial, accessory to that.

That's enough for now, but I wanted you to glimpse the scope of it all. And to give credit where it is due. Thank you, Carl and Eugene. You changed the world.

In Practice

The use of body awareness might be a completely new idea to some readers, and certainly very undeveloped (or simply not valued) by many more, and so we will take time to help you develop this skill. The first thing is to realize that it includes hilariously ordinary body signs, as well as those with more profound implications. They can't be separated, because your body is a unitary system. But they are all things you need to know to be integrated in your daily life.

Let's take a practical example. It just happens I am writing this section of the book in a library. I came down to the cafe for a sandwich, and then I kept writing at my table. It's tempting to stay put and keep going; it's riveting stuff! But the chair in the cafe is very hard, and uncomfortable. Before long, whether I notice it or not, I will begin to write less amiably, or want to

*Every inch of your body is mind.
And realizing this opens up another far
more stunning possibility – that every
inch of everything is mind.*

stop. My thought patterns will narrow and dry up. I notice this, and then make a choice. I head back upstairs to the softer chairs. And now, here I am, back in the flow!

(You may not know that some cafes have special chairs actually designed to be hard on your bum. The reason is clear – they don't want you to stay. Lounging blokes in Lycra who long ago finished their skinny cappuccino really should get on their bikes and make room for other people.)

So, again, try this out. Notice right now your own body in the seat where you are. The odds are a hundred to one you are holding yourself in a slightly uncomfortable posture, because even the act of sitting itself is not what we were designed for, and we need to move to feel good. The point is – you were not aware of that. And it was affecting your mood. Take a deeper breath. Let your shoulders drop. Soften your belly. Shift a little in your chair so you are more aligned. (Or go and take a pee if you need to, don't be like a sheep.) And your mood will improve.

The Social Level

Lest I sound like the bum-comfort awareness ambassador, let's now take this into much more edifying and important territory. As you go through your social day, relating to family or work-mates, your body is constantly, in real time, assessing the situation and giving you a reading.

There are a number of ways it does that. Again, you can start with a simple, almost ridiculous experiment. If you are alone right now, try exclaiming the word 'yes'. If you can manage, do it with emphasis. So, 'Yes!' Now notice what other sensations or experiences seem to accompany this. In your face, chest or elsewhere. If you are reading this on a train or a plane, or beside your partner in bed, perhaps just imagine doing the exercise!

When you've tried that a couple of times, try the opposite. Say the word 'no', or, with feeling, 'No!' And again notice what happens in your body, face or any other place, including your mood or thoughts. For almost everyone who tries this, there is a sense of contraction, of tightening with a 'no', and a lightening and expanding with a 'yes'. If you like an advanced challenge, try saying 'no' with a 'yes' feeling, or the reverse. (Readers prone to being passive-aggressive will find this comes rather easily!) We can say no with open hearts too. In our first book, *The Secret of Happy Children*, my wife Shaaron and I explained the trick of the 'soft' no, which reduces tension when refusing your child's requests – say, for some sweets in the supermarket aisle. It's hard to escalate with someone who is saying no, but only softly and lovingly!

As you start to pay more attention, you will find your body says its own 'yes' or 'no' to almost everything. Every single sentence uttered by another person, for real, on TV or in writing, elicits in your body a basic assent or dissent, a yes or no reaction somewhere inside you. So this is how your body communicates. Firstly, it either contracts, or relaxes. Also, it either feels enlivened or dulled (which involve subtly being taller, or more slumped, as well as changes to heartbeat and circulation, blood vessels opening up, or closing down). When human beings are very happy, they jump up and down, and you can energize yourself by doing just that. Even smiling releases serotonin, the happiness chemical we need for health and wellbeing.

Your body also slides up and down the anxiety scale, from freaked out to calm. It can feed the hormones of anxiety into annoyance and anger if it perceives key aspects (like, is this person bigger or smaller, more or less powerful than me?). Your voice changes pitch. Radio presenter and columnist Richard Glover observed in his book *The Mud House* that he has a special deep voice for talking to tradesmen and people in country pubs.

How can you make practical use of all this? The broad answer will please you. It will recur over and over in this book: you don't have to do anything. You just have to notice. Your body–mind system will do the rest. By leaving, momentarily, the thinking floor of your mansion and going down to the ground floor and looking around, you start to have more information, which will automatically change you without you making any effort. This will start to happen naturally and of itself. This person is annoying me, or I am uneasy about this request to borrow my car/house/money. I was about to agree to this, but it doesn't feel right.

Paying attention to your body helps you to calm down. Noticing, consciously, that you are really anxious (say, as you are about to make a speech or approach a problem with someone you need to talk to) is helpful, because it was there anyhow, but now you have a handle on it. It helps if you, for just a few seconds, pay more attention to that bodily signal. For example, if you are feeling some anxiety symptoms, a shortness of breath or a fluttering heartbeat, just stand still for a moment and feel those sensations. There is a universal sequence that happens when you do this. At first, the sensations will seem to grow stronger; just by virtue of us paying closer attention, we notice them more vividly. This can be disconcerting, but stay with it. Always, a second or two later, they will begin to lessen, almost as if we are digesting the sensations away, absorbing them into the rest of our body. If you are having trouble, you can help the process by also noticing your feet pressing on the ground, or the chair supporting your bottom and back. The parts of your body that actually feel okay will help to soothe the places that don't.

Every time I give one of my talks, I have a small panic attack while I am sitting waiting to start. In fact, I go and sit somewhere quiet just so I can have it in private! A small rush of adrenaline hits me, and I just smile and notice it, because it always goes away. Speaking to an auditorium full of people – some of whom have travelled many miles and have many needs and hopes for their family – is naturally a pressured situation. It would be crazy just to walk onstage and do it without some adrenaline. Even if something goes badly wrong in the talk – a microphone fails, or someone leaps to their feet to testify for Jesus, goes into labour, starts to fight with their spouse (all of which have happened), or I get dizzy or forget what I was going to say – then it's just the same. You just feel it. Keep breathing. It gets momentarily worse, then it goes away.

Using the body – going down to the ground floor – is good in emergencies when you need to help other people, too. Perhaps a person you care about, or a child in your care, is freaking out, they are agitated or distressed, not making much sense. (In the old days, they would have been given a slap.) Ask them to sit down, and to slow their breathing. Ask them what is happening in their body. What are they experiencing on the inside? They will say things like, 'My heart is racing', 'I feel so tight in my chest', or 'My legs want to run away'. As they answer your question, they will travel down, out of their head, into their body, and will automatically start to calm. It will take a few moments. They are becoming what we term 'grounded', and as this happens, you can talk, and they can think, more clearly. But, until you get them down into the basement where all that steam has built up, you will get no sense out of them, and they will not feel safe.

GROUNDING

If anxiety doesn't go away right away, you can do something called grounding, which essentially gets you down into your ground floor using direct sensory input. First of all, just notice three things you can see, notice a bit of detail – really *see* them.

Then notice two things you can hear and one thing you can smell. Dwell on each of these for a second or two, so that you really do perceive them, not merely tick them off. Then feel the temperature of the air on your face, and finally, for good measure, the pressure of your feet on the ground. You will suddenly be present. Stay with that feeling, and within a second or two you will feel it like a settling inside your body, like leaves falling or the snow drifting downwards in a silent forest. Your breath will become slower and more rounded. Anxiety will settle towards calm. Grounding is emergency first aid, and it's a great thing to teach to children.

ANXIETY – AND HOW TO LET GO OF IT

Anxiety, as you probably know, is a huge problem today. The causes are multiple and complex – from gut flora to being on the spectrum and baffled by social interactions, to trauma and the hurry and worry of being on social media. Anxiety is a key aspect of being human, as it's a signal that we have overwound ourselves and need to let things calm. There are a number of ways to do that.

Stop the Overload of Information

Electronic media is a very unnatural phenomenon; it mesmerizes us but tricks our Stone Age nervous system into thinking what we're seeing is happening to us.

It's bizarre that we use scary real-world events – the news and current affairs – as a kind of entertainment, which many families simply have got used to screening continually in their living space.

Social media – again, exploiting our natural wish to connect – brings a yabbering and uncaring, if not downright hostile, crowd of strangers into our bedroom or living room. Our mental ecosystem, meant to comprise a dozen or so members of a hunter-gatherer clan who we naturally need to get along with, suddenly has swelled to hundreds or even thousands of people judging us.

And together both of these things replace the rhythms of nature – and the sensory soothing of natural sights and sounds, plants, animals, a chance to move our bodies vigorously outdoors, and have time and peace to just reflect. We are a big sensitive mammal, and this is not how we are meant to live.

All these things hype us up. They are especially bad for growing children. I described this in my *Raising Girls* book: one in five of all teenage girls in the Western world will spend time on anxiety medication. And boys are not far behind, though they will more likely show their anxiety through aggression or anger.

We can make our environment much, much better for our brains by changing these things – less stimulation, reassuring routines to our lives (the brain loves predictability), music and movement, even singing can help our brain cool down because it has a pattern and repetition that settles us.

Deeper Strategies

For some emergency help with anxiety, here are two quite different but very effective approaches, from The School of Life founder Alain de Botton, and from pioneering anxiety healer Dr Claire Weekes.

Alain de Botton is an interesting man. He believes (and I think he is right) that anxiety is often something we do inside our heads, *instead of something even more scary*. That in effect it's a distraction, a displacement activity. A kind of wheel spinning. He puts the idea as a question . . .

'If I wasn't currently filling my mind with these anxious thoughts, what would I have to think about right now instead?'

He helpfully gives some examples:

'I might realize how sad and lonely I am.'

'I might realize how angry at my partner I am.'

'I might realize how abandoned I feel.'

Most people will resonate with at least one of those three. The thing is, those are very uncomfortable things to realize, and a lot of emotions come to the fore. But when you use the Four-Storey Mansion, you soon discover that emotions are okay, they do their job and they tell us where we need to go. They can't harm us. (When we were kids, our parents often behaved as if emotions were to be avoided at all costs – great gaping holes we would fall in and never climb out of.) Let me repeat, emotions won't hurt you, but *not feeling them might*.

Anxiety resembles a kind of low-grade chronic fear, and partly that's true, but what you are afraid of might just be yourself. Alain invites us to trade in our anxiety for a different and more worthwhile kind of suffering – one that gets you somewhere. He invites us to trade our anxiety for 'a confrontation with the real ambivalence and complexity of life'. So there!

If this is not helpful, then Claire Weekes might be the person for you. Dr Weekes is seen by many therapists as the best person on anxiety of the last century – and she lived through most of it. A pioneering woman scientist, who then trained as a doctor and herself suffered from crippling anxiety, she was very motivated to heal herself. She observed that there are two stages in any panic attack. First, the rush of fear in certain situations, which in fact we all have when out of our comfort zone. This is simply a natural thing that can happen to anyone with a sensitive nervous system (which ordinarily is a good thing to have). But because we have such poor understanding of emotions, people become at first bewildered: What's wrong with me? Am I having a heart attack? Am I going to go crazy? And then, quite naturally, they are panicked by these thoughts. They panic about being panicked. And it's this second wave of self-created panic that makes the symptoms stick around. Instead of staying with the fear process so that it can naturally dissipate, anxious people block it by trying to make it stop.

It's like trying to calm water by slapping it.

Claire found that the old methods of behaviour therapy were clearly wrong. Trying to relax away the fear meant that it was struggled with, rather than allowed.

She advised a four-step approach:

1. **Face it.** Do go into situations that make you feel anxious (as long as they are safe) and don't be afraid of having a panic attack. You actually need to have them to get used to them, to discover for yourself that it really doesn't matter. (Important note: Today, therapists would argue for not forcing yourself into situations that terrify you, but having a support person, and taking it in small steps, even imagining it at first, and letting your body get used to the waves of adrenaline. You can use your four storeys to digest and allow the panic to dissipate.)

2. **Accept** the feelings of panic (or, in other words, just observe all the things your body is doing – shaking, heart racing, blurry vision and so on). Don't fight them or worry about them. (Of course, if you are driving or on a busy street, you might have to pull over and stop for a minute or two!) Let it pass through you, just being aware of it as pure sensation. Weekes writes, 'acceptance is a definite physiological process that eventually soothes'. This will take time and multiple experiences because 'it takes time for the new mood of acceptance to be felt as peace'.

3. Once the panic has been allowed to come fully on, **float** through it. She describes this as not tensing up or becoming rigid, but instead, as much as you can, loosening your muscles, almost so that you 'sag'. Take a deep breath and let it out slowly, several times. And just imagine yourself floating, like a cloud, through the experience. You don't try to stop the experience of panic, you just kind of separate from it.

4. **Let time pass**. Your body will complete the adrenaline rush and naturally settle back down. Don't stress about how long it takes. Gradually, the episodes will reduce.

Dr Weekes is clear that this will take time, as it's a big change of attitude, and a rewiring of your brain to go along with that. Fretting about 'Am I better now?' is not the way to go. The best approach is 'It doesn't matter how long it takes, because the panics don't matter. They soon pass.'

Tens of thousands of people see Claire Weekes as having saved their lives. Her books and audiotapes, with their grandmotherly and caring but sensible tone, are still a wonderful resource.

One final thing: anxiety is not always psychological in cause. It can definitely be the result of real and harmful living circumstances – the impossible demands of a job or a role in the family, an unhappy marriage, a poor living environment or no time or space to feel at peace. And so, as Alain de Botton said at the start, you might discover that something in your life needs to change. It isn't all in your head.

Listen to your own body often, as you go through your day. It's fun, and interesting, and it will tell you more and more truths about yourself and your life. You will notice – and then admit to – misgivings long before they turn into serious issues. A topic will be mentioned, and, every time it is, you will have a twitch in your temples, or a rising of your hackles, or a lurch of fear in your gut. Or perhaps you will sense a heat in your loins, or a leap in your heart – not all topics are unpleasant ones!

Use these sensations as a guide to how you 'really feel' behind the polite exterior. When someone asks how you feel about an idea, plan, decision – where to go on holiday, an expensive purchase, what job to take, whether this doctor is right for you – let your body make a judgment, and factor that in. Your language will change. You'll start saying, 'I don't feel right about that for some reason; let me have a think', or 'I'm not comfortable with the idea, but I can't put my finger on it yet. I'll get back to you.'

Your family and your kids will soon be using this language too. It will begin to hone their intuition and ability to think well. One day, your son or daughter will be on holiday with friends, in Amsterdam or Bangkok or Chicago. It's late, they've been drinking. They are about to get into a car. Holding the car door with one hand, bottle in the other, they will say to their companions, 'You know, I really am tired. I might go up to the room and get an early night.' And something awful that might have happened, doesn't happen.

One Last Thing

There is one last thing. Some of us have been so conditioned by our upbringing that we are in denial of our bodily states completely. We think we are okay, but only because we are numbed out. Men often do this because of being told to be brave from a young age, or women from having been told to put others first. Sometimes we need a kick in the pants from someone to even notice how we are faring.

I have a dear friend who notices very early if I am in a good place or not. She is autistic, and so her concern is half for me and half for herself; she doesn't feel good around unexpressed brooding emotions – they baffle her and make her afraid.

My young friend says, with real concern, 'You are not happy'. 'Yes I am,' I proclaim. 'I am fine.' 'No, you are not'. And then I admit, after some fishing around inside myself, that, well, yes, I do feel a bit out of sorts. And in fact, I do have some small worries. In fact, as we talk, they are quite big worries. And we talk about how I might go about addressing them. 'I knew it,' she will say, then be quite relaxed!

This is in effect what therapists do. Supported by someone else's genuinely caring – and gently penetrating – enquiry, the patient goes inside (to the sensations in their body) and admits, well, yes, they are (sad, angry, scared, excited, in love, ready for adventure), and off they go and do something about it. Helping human beings match up their own insides, get their ducks in a line, is really the most important thing we can do for them. (Apart from cook them a nice meal or mind their kids). But it's handy if you can do it for yourself, and once begun, you mostly will.

YOUR BODY REFLECTION EXERCISES
ONE TO FOUR

1. People vary hugely as to how body-aware they are. If you had to choose a category, would you say you are:

    a) Very shutdown and unaware of your body.

    b) About average, aware sometimes but not always.

    c) Very in touch with sensation, movement, being comfortable in and aware of your body almost all the time.

    One of the key things our body does is demand our attention, since we cannot function if it is not properly taken care of. It does this sometimes by experiencing pain, or by malfunctioning in some way that we cannot ignore. It can be anything from indigestion to knee problems, headaches to sore necks.

2. Do you respond and do something when your body sends you signals? Do you stop and have a rest or nap when you are tired? Move about when you are stiff? Or do you normally override your body and plough on?

3. Do you have parts of your body that hurt or seem to not work very well, recurrently or frequently? (Be very clear here that there are also medical reasons why this might be so. In either case, it's important to find out and then, if necessary, get medical help.)

    Your body awareness can be as simple as noticing fatigue, or a tummy ache from rushing your food and swallowing air, or as complex as a held-in chest or tight throat from having had a violent or damaged parent that you had to deal with as a child.

4. Do you think you might have body conditions that are a legacy of tough times that haven't properly healed?

   Go up to your third floor – thinking – and give yourself some gentle encouragement; you have survived and thrived this far, and you are intelligently addressing your life's issues. With the tools in this book, you may find you can speed up the healing and understanding and be much more loving towards and aware of your body in future.

4

THE SECOND FLOOR

Emotions and How They Power Your Life

In the springtime of 1987, we were expecting a baby. We already had a three-year-old little boy, and this was a much-awaited second child. But four months into the pregnancy, my wife suddenly went into labour. Full of fear, we rushed to the hospital. All I remember of that time now is Shaaron standing in the shower, weeping, with tiny pieces of matter, jelly-like tissue, coming out of her body, and myself, fully clothed but heedless of the wet, reaching in to both support her and to grasp at those pieces for any sign of our hoped-for child. It was sad, and terrible, though at the time I was focused on comforting her, in my barely adequate way, and managing the practicalities. That was on a Friday afternoon, and the next day I was booked to run a training weekend with fourteen people, intense and full of need. I did tell them, in the course of the weekend, what had just happened to us, but my job was to be there for them and that's what I did.

In the weeks that followed, I just became numb. The joyful road we had been on towards having a new baby had disappeared into a void. Shaaron withdrew into her own space, and when I asked her, that was what she wanted to do. Time seemed frozen, life was grey, and days turned into weeks. Then, one afternoon, I went out to the seminar room we had built on our farm, a beautiful chapel-like space. I took my guitar from its hook and sat cross-legged on the floor, sunlight streaming in. I did what lots of musicians do in an idle moment: I just let the songs choose themselves. Some random chords resolved themselves into the Rolling Stones/Melanie Safka song 'Ruby Tuesday', and I began to sing it softly to myself.

And I was gone. Great keening sobs broke out of me; my eyes didn't just cry, they streamed with tears; I bent over my guitar so far my head almost touched the ground, rocking to and fro. The lyrics were not intended, I am sure, to describe our situation, but the mind is a wonderful thing. I knew what I had lost, now: it was a girl, a daughter, and the grief was so profound. I had simply no idea.

Even writing this, thirty years on, I can still feel those emotions, and I am grateful that I was able to release and ride with them, and become more alive, not more deadened, through learning more about my own heart. I have a wonderful daughter now, and Shaaron and I have learned to be closer through hard times. I have also learned some things about helping men with grief. Out of that time came my book *Manhood*, which has helped other men to make healing journeys of their own. Clearly it pays to have a guitar, or at least a song, handy at all times.

Emotions are as central to being human as breathing, or walking. We are all feeling emotions constantly, and new research is showing that even our dreams – often intensely emotional – are an essential part of smoothing out and resolving our anxieties and fears. Emotions are 'a response on the inside to something that happens on the outside', designed to power us through a situation of unusual intensity (bad or good), so that we can return to balance. Until recently, astonishingly few people, including many psychiatrists, really understood why we have feelings, and for several hundred years, northern European cultures like the British tried living without them. The result was a lot of misery, and quite a lot of boredom!

Emotions are the source of our vitality, and drivers of meaning, and thankfully, at last, we are learning to embrace them. This chapter will welcome you to the vibrant and multi-hued dance floor that is the second storey of your Four-Storey Mansion – where your heart dwells and your life force is bursting to be let free.

How Emotions Work, and Why We Have Them

When many people think of emotions, they see them as a problem. But making friends with them shows us how they can be very helpful. Here is how they work.

Imagine this. Your day begins like any other. You wake up, have breakfast, plant goodbye kisses on your loved ones and set off for work. Soon you are zooming down the road in your car, lost in thought. Then, suddenly, something ahead of you catches your eye. A car in the oncoming lane has somehow lost control and is now in your lane, skidding, tyres screeching, heading right at you.

Every muscle in your body tightens, you hit the brakes, eyes wide, shouting your favourite expletive! With really nowhere to escape, you just have time to think, Oh no! and then, amazingly, just feet away, the driver swerves back into their own lane, and passes by unscathed. There is nothing much you can do but drive on. Vibrating like a struck gong, you manage to get to work, where you have trouble holding your coffee cup steady.

The odd thing in this story is that – in a sense – nothing happened. You didn't die, you didn't even scratch your car. Yet a lot happened psychologically. Your brain has registered that you could have died or been seriously injured and your life forever changed. You stared death in the face, had to take action very suddenly, beyond your usual experience. And then it was all over.

But you now carry some residual 'charge' in your body that needs to be dealt with. Remember what an emotion is – *it's a change on the inside, in response to an event on the outside.* And it's a necessary and useful change. It's as if a lightning bolt has struck you, and now you are carrying that electricity inside of you. (It's actually a big burst of hormones like adrenaline, noradrenaline, cortisol or endorphins, but let's stick with the electricity metaphor, because that's what it feels like – you are charged up!)

Since the cars didn't collide after all, and there was no need to do anything about it, you are left in a rather odd place. You have this sudden excess of energy in your system with nowhere to go. When you get to work, you will probably try to discharge that energy by talking. 'You wouldn't believe what happened to me . . .' On returning to your loved ones, you may give them the full details. If you are an emotionally open person, and those around you are trustworthy and caring, you might burst into tears, or ask for a hug, and shudder or shiver as you let go of the stored-up 'charge' in your body. You will let out little bits of the 'lightning' all day long.

If you don't do this, or don't have the chance, *the charge will remain in your body*. And it will add to other undischarged emotions you may have had. This accumulation of unexpressed feelings is what we call post-traumatic stress disorder, or PTSD – the stress that is left behind after the trauma is gone. But here is the odd thing – we human beings are *designed for trauma*. Life was often rather scary and dramatic for our ancestors, and we evolved to handle that by letting our feelings out. In many cultures, people sob and cry and comfort each other after anything bad has happened, and they speak from their hearts much more than we do, and so they can cope with a great deal. And the old cultures also made the time and space to do that.

PTSD is not a natural consequence of trauma; it happens when there have been serious incidents one on top of another, without a chance to heal. Because our culture hasn't paid

attention to this, it's become a massive health problem for
millions of people, often the ones who do the most valuable
– but dangerous – work on our behalf, such as emergency
workers, peacekeepers, soldiers, the police, journalists, doctors
and nurses. For years, the culture around these professions
was to not show any emotions, and that turned out to have
been the worst thing possible. Ancient cultures, from the Maori
to the Greeks, had rituals and ceremonies deliberately to help
rehumanize their warriors. We only offered beer.

To prevent PTSD happening to you, the first thing to
remember is that your emotions were natural, and in fact
might have been needed. Had your cars both screeched to a
halt, inches away from colliding, and a couple of teenagers got
out and laughed at you, you may well have punched one of
their lights out, in the spirit of community parenting. It would
have helped you feel better, as it dealt with the anger aspect
of having been so witlessly put at risk. Perhaps more helpfully,
if you had spoken sternly to them and refused to leave without
calling the police, it would have made the world a safer place.
It would have been weak and unhelpful to simply let the incident go. Anger is needed to be strong, and focused, and we
all need to have some in ready reserve. If a collision had taken
place, your emotions would have been needed then, too. With
your car hit and in flames, you might need to fight your way
out of the wreckage, run to safety, or get help for injured or
trapped people. The adrenaline would make you remarkably
strong and fast. Fear would have been your friend, energizing
you and making you 'feel no pain' as you did what was needed.

Worst of all, if someone had been killed, an innocent bystander, say, then your arrival at the office would have been in a very different vein. Shock and grief, and intensely slowed-down feelings, would have made it difficult for you to do your work. You would probably have needed to go home and would have been in need of some counselling.

But the thing is (and this is a challenging idea, I know), that whole terrible incident, if handled properly, and processed fully by your body, would *have eventually become a useful and life-affirming experience.* You would have been enlarged, and a kinder and wiser person ever after. My clients often tell me, towards the end of the healing process from very severe events, that they do not regret what happened, because of what they learned about life. In fact, that is really a good indicator that they are healed.

Post-Traumatic Growth

Knowing how fragile life is – that death is always close by – is a core insight for a wise and well-lived life. A friend of mine is a renowned journalist, who took pride in being in dozens of nightmarish situations until, one day, the inevitable happened and he imploded with anxiety symptoms – intrusive thoughts, nightmares, uncontrollable rages and tsunamis of guilt and fear. Unable to find the help he needed even in the best treatment facilities, he self-educated himself on trauma healing.

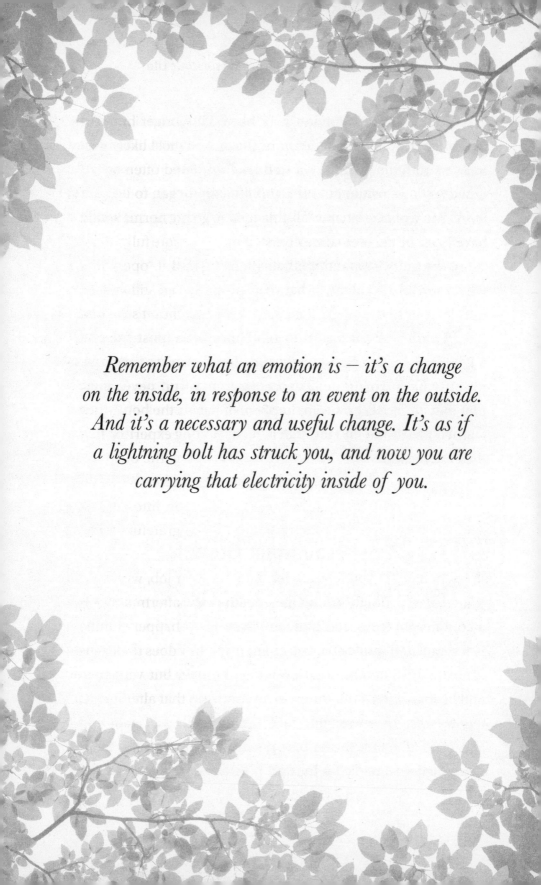

*Remember what an emotion is — it's a change
on the inside, in response to an event on the outside.
And it's a necessary and useful change. It's as if
a lightning bolt has struck you, and now you are
carrying that electricity inside of you.*

He did so because otherwise he would no longer have been able to function as a father or husband and most likely would have taken his own life – a step he considered often because of the sheer torment of his symptoms. He began to learn that there is a place beyond all this, but it is not normality. It is both a spiritual and a cognitive step to being more fully human. The Buddhist teacher Stephen Levine called it 'opening the heart in hell'. You know what you know, but can still decide to trust, and love, and be at ease. It's not easy, but it's real.

Therapists have begun to refer to this as 'post-traumatic growth'. My very first message to the therapists I train is to stop pathologizing their trauma patients, and never merely to aim for 'getting back to normal'. Normal is the booby prize, and if you have been through a heart-searing experience, you should never waste it by going back to being 'the old you'. In fact, you can't. Push on, and let it take you higher. What point is there in suffering except to let it turn you into someone who deeply cares for others and is intensely grateful for being alive?

Emotions, if you learn to let them do their job, will get you through the situation, and then through the aftermath, as you continue to learn and grow from what has happened. It can be absolutely profound: you are mortal. How does that change your plans? It can be an everyday thought, but very useful: people can do dumb things in traffic. Does that alter how you should drive? And so on.

So emotions are vital processes that help you through an event and afterwards. They help you reassemble your sense of self in the world. But what are they? How do they work? That's something every human being at every age needs to know about themselves. Here goes . . .

The Big Four Emotions

Emotions come with being a mammal – and some, like sorrow and grief, go with being an advanced animal that can remember (even elephants and great apes feel grief). And you will be pleased to know that emotions are very simple. Like primary colours, every hue and shade of human emotion is mixed from a handful of primary emotions. There are just four basic feelings: joy, anger, sorrow and fear. Everything else – all the complex emotions human beings manage to have, like jealousy, nostalgia, envy and, of course, love – are combinations of these four. Mixed feelings, though, can pull us in different directions, and that makes them hard to get to the bottom of. For example, jealousy is anger combined with fear. But anger sends a message of back off, while fear asks a person to come closer. Not surprisingly, this mixture is almost always a disaster. If we are jealous, it's better to voice the fear and resolve it one way or the other. Whenever feelings are mixed, one will be 'primary', and, by staying with that one, you are more likely to find a way through.

What a good therapist will do is help you to take those complex mixtures of emotion back to their basic ingredients and tackle each one in turn. It's not a bad way to tackle anything that has you unsettled or upset. Sit down and write it down – in this situation, what are you sad about? What are you angry about? What are you afraid of? What do you feel good about? This will often bring surprising insights and also be very cathartic and may help you to know what to do next. Usually one of those four will be stronger than the others, and that will be the one to attend to first. Then perhaps another will come to the surface more. Feelings, once attended to, begin to sort themselves and balance out. Gradually, as we will show you in the following pages, you will untangle yourself.

I once watched some beautiful therapy by my teachers Bob and Mary Goulding. A young man was talking about being afraid to show his true self to a potential partner. Asked why, he said, 'In case I am rejected.' Mary Goulding, a gutsy seventy-year-old, with an accent like a New York cab driver, said, 'But if she doesn't like the real you, you're better off knowing straight-up? You can say goodbye and move on!' And as she could see that idea 'sinking in', she smiled warmly. 'There are plenty of positive, warm-kinds-of women in the world just busting to find a good-hearted man.' And she turned to the women in the watching audience and noted the nods and smiles.

Each primary feeling has a job to do. Let's start with the simplest, and most primitive. Fear helps us to be safe, it prevents us from doing risky or deadly things. If we can get away, then that takes care of the problem. When we are afraid in an ongoing way – something we have to face – we need people to support us. A hug is a good start as it reassures our body – I have allies and help right here. Our brain then comes in – we need to get information and make a plan to rebuild some structure for dealing with what has come along. To slow down and think things through. When it is reassured that we have got the right things in place, the fear subsides. It has done its job.

Anger is also pretty straightforward. Its job is to energize us to defend our space, to stand our ground, or keep our identity from being swallowed. Angry people need to be given space. To have their message heard. To be taken seriously. It's not, though, a licence to be scary or violent – we'll come back to that a bit further on.

Often the key with managing our own anger is to learn to speak up early, not wait until we are really angry. Experienced parents will play-act that they are angry to rouse their kids along, raising voices or speaking sharply, but with no real hostility. (The kids feel it on both levels – their brain says, 'We'd better hustle,' but in their supersense they don't feel unsafe.) Asked to think of an angry person, most people picture a large red-faced male, looming and threatening. But this is dysfunc-tional anger, anger being misused. In a healthy person, anger can be loud, it can be clear, but it shouldn't endanger anyone else. It should simply be used to establish some boundaries, and that can be done quite calmly.

Sorrow is more gradual and profound. Its purpose is to ease the process of letting go, when we have no other choice, of people and things precious to us. Again, being able to talk usually starts it off, but as we struggle with the pain of letting go, a trusted person being close, or even holding us as we let the sorrow flow through, will make it easier. And just lots of time out of our normal lives, to grieve and reflect. Amazingly, the act of crying releases pain-reducing hormones in the body, which helps heal the intense mental pain caused by the loss of someone or something in our world. Crying isn't the problem, it's the solution, and it means things have started to get better.

But if grief is something that cannot be avoided, then some surprising things can move it along. Dancing, music, long walks and time to reflect can also help. The worst thing we can do is to seek numbness, and nothing messes up the grief process as much as using alcohol or drugs, or any compulsive activity, to run away from it. It has to be faced. Sorrow is the longest and slowest emotion to resolve, because it involves rewiring large areas of our brain to adjust to the loss. And the outcome will be a growth, not a diminishment. We should not simply move on – that would rob us of something. As we grieve, we are tucking parts of the person or situation away in our brain under the label 'gone but not forgotten', as cherished memories. These memories remain a resource for life. There eventually is a richness and appreciation when we remember the person we once had in our life. Sadness, like all emotions, comes in waves, and those waves settle down to a kind of sweet rocking that reminds us we are alive.

And finally, joy. What is joy all about? Happiness, in all its shades – excitement, pleasure, exhilaration, contentment – helps us celebrate our life and be grateful. We should find ways and opportunities to express or feel joy whenever we can. Dancing, laughing, playing the fool, or just quietly noticing the wonder of the world. Happiness floods our body with hormones that boost immunity, heal damage and help our brain to grow. But who needs a reason?

Emotions are physiological states so strong that we can experience them as truly profound, and their function is both a compass that points towards what we need and an energy source to get us there. There are no 'negative' emotions – they are all intended to help us, protect us and energize our lives. We'd be pretty boring without them; in fact, we couldn't survive at all. The renowned neuroscientist Antonio Damasio found that, when people lose their access to their emotions (through some bad brain accident or surgery), they may be intellectually unharmed, yet they have great trouble making decisions or choosing actions. He tells the tragic story of an eminent scientist who needed the emotion part of his brain to be removed because of a tumour. Afterwards, he would be found by his colleagues at work, simply immobilized over some small decision, such as where to go to for lunch. Emotion helps us decide. This is implicit in the way we speak – I 'feel' like a walk. I 'feel' restless. Emotions help us to know what we value. They team up with our rational thinking to make it somehow more complete, and wise. Though, they can also get out of control and send our thinking haywire, so we should never leave them solely in charge. (More of this later.)

A CHILD IN GRIEF

Life is often hard. There will always be things that make us sad, scared or discouraged. Sometimes, what we need most from those who love us is just that they understand that, and they are there for us . . .

In the playground one morning, five-year-old Darius was looking lonely, and Janelle, the duty teacher, went over to him.

'How are you today, Darius?'

'I'm a bit sad, Miss.'

'What are you sad about?'

'I miss my mum.'

Janelle felt the pit of her stomach fall away. Because, six weeks ago, Darius' mum had died after a long illness. The school knew about this, and had been keeping an eye on the little boy to make sure he was okay. Janelle knew how to make her body steady around emotions; she felt her feet on the ground and breathed, and looked down at this little boy's face. She said, 'What about her are you missing today?' Darius had no trouble answering. 'When I hurt myself, she would kiss it better.' Janelle moved slightly to be alongside him, close but not in his field of view. 'Would you like me to kiss it better? Would that be any help?' He didn't speak, just lifted up a scratched hand from where he had fallen over a few minutes ago. She kissed it softly and looked into his eyes. 'Thanks, Miss,' he said, and immediately ran off to join the other kids.

Janelle knew something important – that *a huge grief is actually made up of many little griefs*. Each takes time to be felt, and known, and cared about. Not everything can be fixed, but everything can be 'held', acknowledged, given its due. Feelings take care of themselves, as they were designed to, but it takes others who care to make that happen smoothly. Cheering someone up, or telling them not to feel that way, or moving too quickly to try to fix something which really can't be fixed, only blocks the process and makes it harder to heal. Human beings can handle dreadful things, but only if those around them stay comfortable with strong feelings and be there for them.

Distinguishing Emotions

Emotions start in the body, but they are more specific and developed than the sensations we talked about on the 'ground floor'. Your daughter's stomach ache might be just indigestion, but it might also mean she is being bullied at school. She is frightened but may not quite know how to tell you that. She needs your help to gently get to the bottom of things. A huge amount of parenting is helping kids with their feelings – not always fixing them, but always listening and caring and allowing them.

Feelings are clusters of body sensations – for example, a clenched jaw, a hot sensation, tight shoulders, a rush of energy to the head and face – that often happen together and signal a specific and distinct thing: an emotion. In this case, anger.

Always remember, an emotion is a *process*; it's something

going somewhere. If you feel stuck in an emotion, something is wrong. Talking it through is almost always helpful. Then use your supersense to find a way through it. Notice where it lives in your body; usually there will be a specific location, often several. We often hold sadness in our eyes or sinuses, anger in our shoulders or jaw, sorrow in our belly, but these are not fixed, as each person varies.

When I learned karate in my teens, we were shown a specific way to form a fist for the most effective impact. When I am threatened (an unfriendly post on Facebook is the worst thing in my universe!), the first sign is that, all of its own volition, my hand makes a fist of itself. My hand seems to know I am angry before I do!

Each emotion has a completely different set of body signs. In an unforgettable scene in *Saving Private Ryan*, a motorcycle messenger brings a telegram to a remote farmhouse. Steven Spielberg filmed this scene from a distance, with no sound, so you do not see anyone's face. A woman in an apron comes to the porch, takes the telegram, reads it and collapses to her knees. That's all you need to see to know what has happened. Grief is primal and universal – an open mouth wailing, deep sobs from the belly, water running from the eyes, a body curving over forwards or falling to the ground. Sadness is a whole-body experience, we can only deal with it by surrendering to it, and letting it do its job.

THE MESSAGE OF MR ROGERS

If you grew up in the UK, Australia, or anywhere else outside the US, then you missed something really worthwhile – the children's television show called *Mr Rogers' Neighborhood*. It ran for thirty-three years and was part of the lives of little kids for a whole generation.

Fred Rogers' work was celebrated in a movie with Tom Hanks (*A Beautiful Day in the Neighborhood*) and an acclaimed and very moving documentary on Netflix, called *Won't You Be My Neighbor?* Watch either of them and you will learn a great deal about how to be human.

Rogers was a newly graduated Presbyterian minister, also qualified in music, who saw his first television at his mother's house, in 1951. He was horrified at the lack of respect for human dignity in the children's fare at the time. And of course it hasn't got much better.

Fred worked with the leading child psychology people of his day to construct a daily TV show about emotions, getting along with people and self-worth. With quaint puppets, a slow, child-friendly rhythm and Rogers' gentle presence, it became one of the most successful programmes in the history of television.

The messages he taught are a foundation for mental health at any age:

1. Focus on the person you are with. Be with them completely. (Rogers, on-screen but also personal magic was that, mentally, he was addressing himself to one single child, pausing for them to understand, beaming goodwill and

gentle respect – you felt that he too had a shy child inside him, but had simply discovered the delights of human connection, and was offering it to you.)

2. Everyone in the world, from tiny children to mass murderers, needs to be loved unconditionally (in fact, when mass murders or terrible things did occur, Rogers was always clear that this was the reason – the perpetrators had not been loved as they needed, and so felt they had to do 'something big'). Rogers addressed children's fears at the times of the Kennedy assassinations, for example; he didn't shy from what he knew they were hearing and dealing with in those turbulent years. He understood the profoundly radical message – probably the most important fact of child development – that only when we feel loved and valued 'as we are' can we unfold into who we might become. That loving children unconditionally (and showing that) is the thing that frees them to grow.

3. We all have a shy and nervous child inside us that easily gets scared or angry, and needs help to manage that. 'What do you do with the mad that you feel?' was a regular theme of the show and the title of one of its most memorable songs. He noted that children attached to toy guns or swords (and one might add politicians or dictators who do the same) were frightened by how weak they felt in the world. And he would tell small boys that they were strong on the inside, which of course they then aspired to be. And to be able to be vulnerable and talk about feelings with someone trusted was braveness itself.

4. Sorrow and grief are totally natural and inevitable in life, but they do diminish, and joy returns. Sorrow can feel

unbearable at the time (many visitors to his programme were children who had lost parents, divorce was a topic he tackled often, and of course children in that era also had many incurable diseases0, but nothing in life couldn't be faced and brought to a human level. Rogers understood that it was human connection that made life bearable, and so we had to talk to kids about their feelings and fears. He put it so simply – 'If it's mentionable, it's manageable.' And it wasn't as hard as all that. You just had to be prepared to have your own heart tugged at as well.

5. And, finally, we adults have a very major job to do – we have to fight against the trashing and exploitation of children that will always be in the world. We have to protect childhood so that it can be the time of unfolding that it was meant to be, and children can grow strong.

Why Do We Find Feelings Hard?

If feelings are so simple, why do we have so much trouble? It's no mystery; the twentieth century – especially the first half – was a nightmare: two world wars, massive depressions, massive refugee flows around the world. Our great-grandparents underwent huge trauma. They often just shut down all emotions, because in an emergency that is what you do. But then they could not come back into the light. They did not understand what we now call 'triggering', and so could not bear the sight or sound of

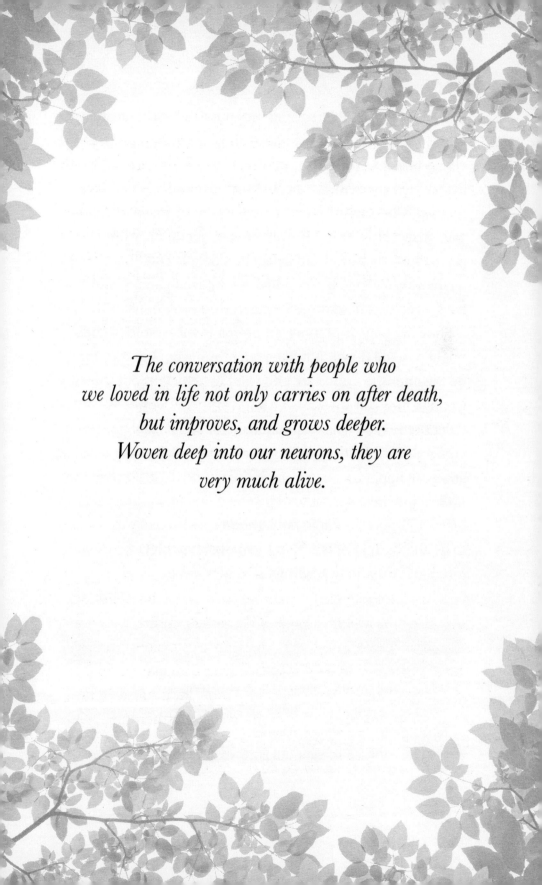

*The conversation with people who
we loved in life not only carries on after death,
but improves, and grows deeper.
Woven deep into our neurons, they are
very much alive.*

emotions in their children, and they punished them for showing them. Our parents were raised by those parents, and while the effects began to wash out, still there were many families where life was too dangerous – alcohol was involved, violent dads, or mothers who simply could not cope, sexual abuse of children was taking place but not ever spoken about. So, even by the generation when we were kids, often people could not handle us showing feelings. If we felt bad and told our parents, they may have given us a hard time, and then we'd feel doubly bad.

Showing your true inner emotions *is* vulnerable; someone might put you down, not like you, or not care. But they might do the opposite – and care and want to help. Without showing feelings, how can anyone even know you? The wonderful story-teller Brené Brown has explained this so well: if you can't show vulnerability, she reasons, if you can't take risks, then nothing good can happen – no love, no intimacy, no trust, no creativity, no real joy. Take a minute to just take that in: *nothing good in life ever happens without vulnerability*. So it's really important to be able to at least talk about your feelings, however uncom-fortable it may be to begin with. It gets easier.

WHY GRIEF IS NOT GOODBYE

Sometimes, an idea that at first is helpful can, in its turn, become something that holds us back. A very good instance of this is the concept of closure.

In the 1970s, a straight-talking Swiss-American psychiatrist called Elisabeth Kübler-Ross drove a truck through the beliefs of her day about death and dying. It's hard now to believe that, just a generation ago, doctors and family members routinely kept a cancer diagnosis secret from the dying patient. Millions of people lived out their last days in an agony of pretending, confusion and emotional distance, because they simply were not told the truth.

I remember the distress of a young woman client of mine who came to work in Australia on a two-year contract, not knowing that, back home in Ireland, her much-loved brother had terminal cancer. His wife and his doctors *kept it a secret from him, and everyone else.* So, one shocking day, my client simply learned that her brother had died. She never got to say goodbye to him. There was not even time to fly home for his funeral.

Kübler-Ross changed things utterly. She convinced the world of the necessity and goodness of having lots of time with the dying person, saying our goodbyes fully and clearing up any unfinished business. That grief was natural and good, and that it progressed through stages which were all a necessary part of letting go. But, along with these good messages, somehow the idea crept in that, one day, grief would be done and dusted. That there would be closure.

Now, closure of course has meaning and value. Today, mothers and fathers of stillborn babies are allowed to hold and keep their deceased infant for as long as they need. To examine their tiny fingers, their faces. To cuddle them and weep together over them. One of the most profound human tragedies is softened, even as it is made intense, and after a day or a week, parents find they are able to let this child go.

By allowing themselves to feel, their hearts have come through.

Closure does not mean forgetting. The idea of stages of grief does not therefore mean that it has an ending, nor even that we would want it to. That would be a profound misunderstanding of what human beings mean to each other. We are not just objects to be discarded when our utility has ended. A relationship does not end when the person is physically gone. Traditional cultures, who knew a great deal about the nature of the mind, were much more engaged with the dead – they kept them emotionally, intellectually, around.

So we need to ask a fundamental question – what if the grief process is not a letting go at all? What if it's an *integration* of a person into your own heart? You may have loved a partner or friend for forty or fifty years. They have immeasurably enriched, comforted and loved you, and you them.

(This certainly applies to me. If I could attribute one single outstanding gift from my own partner, Shaaron, it is that *she has made me a better person*. Through learning to get along with her, listening to how very different her experiences are from mine, growing through innumerable crises and tight spots, the way we just set each other off laughing, I am not even remotely the messed-up shrivelled person I might have been. Everyone who has been helped by my work owes a great debt to her. If she dies before me, do I want to 'get over' her? To have closure? Hell, no!)

The conversation between people who were deeply engaged in life does not just carry on, but improves, deepens and grows, even after death. The astonishing way that we tangle into each other's consciousness means that, as we continue to live and grow, so does our relationship to the person who has died. Many movies have tapped into this idea because the experience of ongoing connection is totally, neurologically real.

For that reason alone, it is worth taking many months, or years, if needed, to sit with the memory, feel the loss, reflect and absorb. To set aside time from all normal preoccupations and enter a liminal time, to walk beaches, be alone, write or create. So we can take these precious people even deeper into our hearts.

How to Use Your Emotions

For all their power and meaning, emotions are still a practical and here-and-now phenomena you can learn to experience more comfortably.

How do you use your emotions? It works like this. In any situation, as often as you can do it, on every day of your life, you listen to your body, just as we learned in the last chapter, and, sure enough, sometimes you will find there are some strong, often unpleasant sensations that are not going away. In fact, they seem to be intensifying. This is your mind's early-warning system saying that something in your mental or outer world needs your attention right now.

For example, imagine that someone has let you down, twice in a row. They look like doing it again. As you focus on this fact, you feel slightly hot and perhaps a little tense in the shoulders. Yep, you are angry, and it makes sense – they are not respecting your needs or boundaries, and it's time to do something, to make changes. You might tell them your feelings, the reason for them and how their behaviour is impacting you. (Thomas Gordon calls this an 'I statement' – I feel___ when you___ because___ and I would like you to___. Yelling expletives at them is impactful, but does not carry much information, and tends to make people defensive!)

In any relationship, boundaries have to be discovered by trial and error. The person you are angry with will either show shame and remorse, and you will supersense that they really intend to change, or they will come across as flaky or slippery, and you will know not to trust them in future. Either way, you are better off and your feelings will abate somewhat.

The anger might take a different course, once you think about it. You might decide this is not an important relationship to you – perhaps one with a tradesperson or supplier – and that you have alternatives. So you might curse and swear and tell a few friends about it, but the most important thing is you just won't use those people again. That decision uses the energy of the anger, in effect, to build a fence, to cut a tie. And it makes your life better. Fritz Perls, the inventor of Gestalt therapy, said that it takes aggression even to eat a carrot! Like penguins in a rookery, sorting out the nesting spaces, it's simply how we get along. A few pecks and people know not to mess with us. Even the closest relationships still have boundaries, and real intimacy is only possible when we define ourselves clearly. So don't freak out if you get cross with someone you love. Be focused on just this problem in the here and now. Don't say, 'You always . . .' or 'You never . . .' Preface your anger with, 'Right now . . .' so it stays manageable. You can be devoted, committed and adoring of someone and still 'right now' find them hugely irritating or insufferable. That is just how relationships are!

An emotion is not something to become lost in or taken over by. Tantrums are for toddlers, and then we are supposed to grow out of them. If anger, or any other emotion, feels overwhelming or has built up for some reason, take it somewhere safe and let it out. Let people know you need some more time to work out how you feel. Take that time, supersense your way into that emotion and get to the bottom of it. Then come back to the topic when you are more grounded and clear. It's possible – and we can all learn – to be angry and still be very calm, safe and clear.

When It's Not Really Anger

There's something very important to know, here. Someone who is angry a lot, such as a violent or controlling partner in a marriage, is almost always not angry, but frightened. His or her childhood history likely involved being abandoned or abused, and so they carry a lot of fear in a very young part of themselves and cover it with anger. Of course, the anger is all we see, so it's natural not to realize where it comes from, and the person himself may be quite unaware of this too. Until they get help, this makes them very dangerous, because people's reactions to their anger add to the underlying fear, which they then turn into even more anger and the cycle builds. We urgently need to get more help to such people, as early in their lives as possible.

Because this conditioning is more often present in men, we need services and programmes that understand that male aggression is coming from a frightened place, and which help those men to own and process their childhood trauma or needs from their past, not get them tangled up with the people in their lives now.

Some of us haven't got much access to our anger, we have been trained into niceness, and it can be remarkably disabling. I was in this category for much of my life. In the 1980s, Shaaron and I and a small group of friends founded the first Youthline telephone service, for suicide prevention in young people, in our part of the world. We gathered a wonderful group of volunteers and trained intensively, but we still needed funds to make it happen.

To raise the money, we contracted to do the gatekeeping and ticket-selling for a local folk festival. I found myself with a team of young people, mostly under twenty-one, getting ready to deal with large crowds, including biker gangs and drunks, for several days and nights, across half a dozen venues. Just as things were getting underway, my main 'lieutenant' – a good friend who had encouraged me in starting the project – came up to me with a group of mates who I did not know. He explained, while they hung back, that he wanted to attend the concerts rather than be stuck taking tickets or looking after our team.

I was about twenty-five years old then, and a very different person from who I am now. I just nodded and said, 'Oh, okay, sure', I didn't say that it would double my stress and responsibilities, and make the young people less safe. And I just let it pass. I feel disbelief, now, that I could have been so spineless. Sometime later, something almost hilariously symbolic took place. A kid's kite got stuck in a tree on our farm. My friend was there, and he held a ladder while I tried to retrieve it. The ladder began to slip, and instead of bracing against it, he simply stepped back and let it fall. Only by jumping clear did I avoid ending up in a tangle of ladder and broken limbs on the hard concrete drive. My friend quite literally 'let me down'.

After that, we were not friends anymore. After years of therapy – psychodrama, Gestalt, bodywork, encounter groups, family therapy training – I had got in touch with my anger! I didn't explode – perhaps I should have; it might have unearthed something important and made something positive come of it – I just sent an email explaining why, and never saw him again.

Anger's first function is self-protection. In relationships, it also has another dimension: it means you care. If someone, a friend or partner, is angry with you, then it means they are still invested in you. They still think the relationship is worth the energy. When we give up on something, which sometimes we must, the emotions diminish too. And that might be just the right thing. There is some sorrow, and then we move on.

Don't Become Your Emotions

The heart of emotional intelligence is to know your emotions and feel them fully, but not mistake them for your whole self. To not get trapped on only one floor of your mansion. Everyone knows someone who emotes their way through life, being constantly what my old mum would call 'in a flap.' And everyone knows an inadequate, often not very bright person who uses anger as a way of being in the world. These are people who feel too much and need to think more. (Of course, some people think too much and need to feel more. It's rather life-transforming to work out which one is you!)

The skill that will grow in you from reading this book is that, little by little, you'll find yourself being a calm observer, someone who moves easily through the rooms of your mansion, never getting stuck in any of them. You'll start to notice anger, fear, sorrow or joy, even when they are just slight beginnings – micro-emotions, if you like. But you'll be able to stand outside of them, as if you are watching small, timid animals emerge into a clearing. Eventually, even in the most intense grief, terror or fury, you will find you can still be a calm bystander, watching. The emotions might be in full flight – you are shouting things that really needed to be expressed, or sobbing wildly on your bed, or in someone's arms, or shuddering at what almost happened, giving full rein, though safely, to your wild animal self. Yet you are also quietly amazed at your own intensity and aliveness: 'Wow!

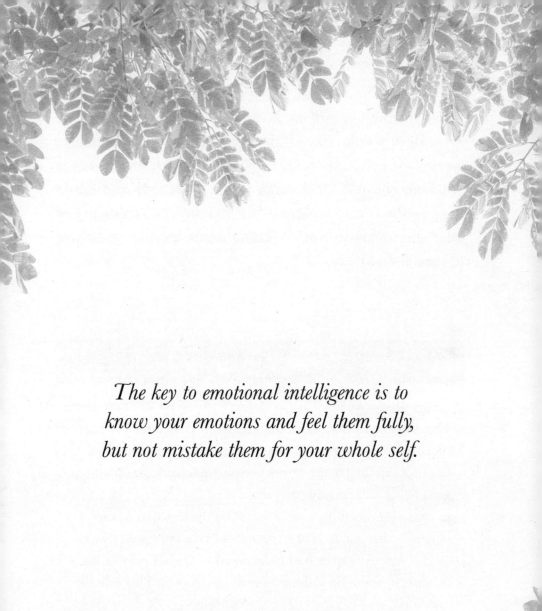

*The key to emotional intelligence is to
know your emotions and feel them fully,
but not mistake them for your whole self.*

Listen to you! Go, girl!' By keeping on noticing that you are in a wider world, staying in your body so that it remains steady, you will let those feelings do their work and pass from you, and you will be through to the other side and find a deep peace. (I can remember the first time I was able to cry, after almost twenty years without doing so. The peace was beyond belief.)

PLEASE LISTEN TO WHAT I AM NOT SAYING

Many years ago, my main work was training counsellors, and one weekend I flew to an outback town in Australia to train doctors from the region. We spent the first day learning the skills of listening to the whole person, their feelings, situation, and being able to gain their trust.

The next morning, one of the older doctors had a story to share. Overnight, he'd been on roster in the emergency ward, and a young woman had been flown in from a remote out-station, in premature labour. She was at risk of birthing months too soon, and likely to need another emergency flight on to a capital city. But there was time to talk to her, and he sat with her and put some of his new-found skills to the test.

She told him that she lived on a very isolated farm with her husband and his mother, and that the mother was highly critical, endlessly finding fault. With the approach of a new baby, this had only increased, and she was deeply unhappy. The doctor sat with her as this story poured out, mostly just listening, rather shocked that a patient would tell him such personal things.

To his surprise, while they talked, the contractions she had been having slowed, and then stopped altogether. The emergency flight was put on hold and, by morning, she was stable and resting. The hospital team decided that they would give her the option to remain in the town for the rest of her pregnancy, for the safety of herself and the baby, and she wept with relief. The doctor, a crusty no-nonsense kind of man, was elated that he had found some new tools to help his patients.

Acknowledging the mystery that other people are, we treat them very differently. And they reveal themselves more fully as well. Everything goes better.

In Conclusion

Even a normal day in our lives can give us bits of leftover emotion. So, whenever you can, resolve those emotions by going down to your ground floor, and deal with them as sensations. Notice where the feeling is being held – belly, shoulders, throat, or somewhere else in your body. Then soften and be aware of the region surrounding the stuck feeling. Give that held energy more space to breathe and expand. Notice that in fact the emotion is starting to move – to grow, or shift in your body, or to dissolve. Soon you will learn to do this in real time; while having a conversation or other experience, you can breathe and process the emotions and let them inform

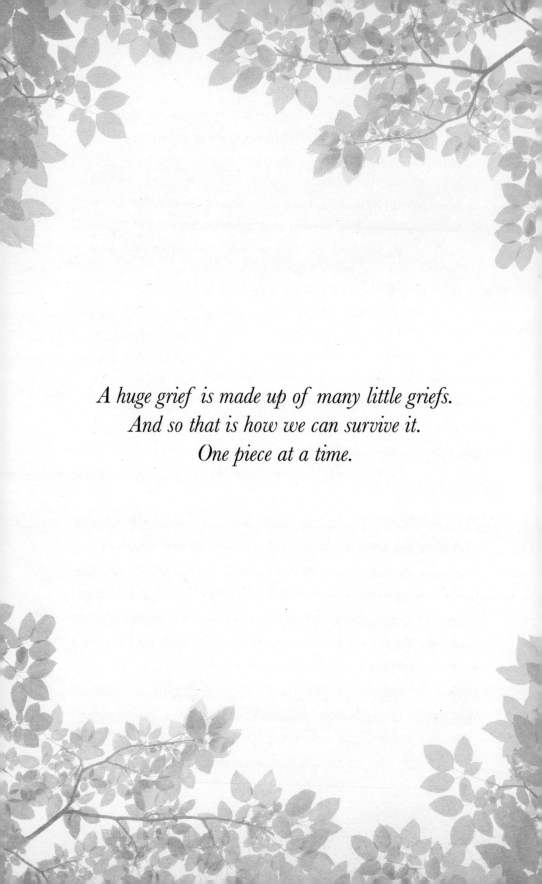

A huge grief is made up of many little griefs.
And so that is how we can survive it.
One piece at a time.

you. You'll begin to say things like, 'I feel uneasy about that idea', or 'I don't feel right about that just yet, let me have a day to think it over.' And you act accordingly. Feelings are an energy source to make changes. But, if they seem to be excessive or clearly 'left over' then find a way to discharge them, like ammunition that's no longer needed, it's dangerous to leave them lying around!

You might need to wait until you have time and space. Then simply let yourself do whatever your body wants to, in safe ways. Cry, pound a mattress, cuddle your pillow, shout if nobody is around. Notice if specific words come out of you. Be objectively interested in your own healing wisdom carrying you along. It may be dramatic, or totally easy, like the sun coming out of the clouds. It's always worthwhile. Maturity means not carrying emotions over once they have done their job. You have released them, and you can breathe easy again.

Millions of parents suffer miscarriages, just as Shaaron and I did back forty years ago. It is an important life event and one that has to be worked through. Because I was able to grieve, my emotions carried me through this process. As a result, I was not fearful of trying for another baby. Shaaron and I were able to grow closer again, and I didn't stay locked in a frozen shell of 'toughing it out', which was really just hiding from the pain that goes with life. I was able to open my heart to our daughter, and granddaughters, and know that life is so fragile, but so resilient, that having an open heart is the only way to live in this world.

I hope this chapter has been illuminating and helped you to feel better! Emotions add to the huge riches of information that our body is giving us. They give us power and energy. But they are also rather like beautiful, innocent, giant children, scrapping and bawling their way through life. And children need an adult, somewhere around. We clearly need something else – a clear head and a sense of purpose. And that takes us up to the next floor. The intellect. The brain in your head. The place where meaning can be found.

YOUR EMOTIONS – REFLECTION EXERCISES ONE TO SIX

1. Some of us simply do not notice our emotions, or only do so when they explode out of us. Would you say you were:
   a) Easy and comfortable with your emotions.
   b) Comfortable with some and not others.
   c) Rather unemotional and wooden, not aware of them much at all.

2. Some of us run our minds at a high level of agitation and are full of emotion of an intense kind a lot of the time. We don't either ground in our body or slow down and think clearly enough in our heads. Is your experience of emotions one of being 'caught in them' and often overcome with fear, anger or sorrow?

3. Which of the four emotions are you most comfortable with: anger, sorrow, fear or joy?

4. Which one do you most repress or not feel, even in circumstances when it would help you to have that energy or expression? Which feeling, in other words, are you most likely to 'bottle up'? If you go down to your ground floor of your mansion, can you feel where in your body that emotion tends to be stored?

5. Do you think that particular past experiences have stayed locked inside you, that you suffer from PTSD? (We'll come to this in the next chapter, just answer yes or no here!)

6. Are you able to witness calmly your own emotions, and accept and guide them so they find their place and do their job?

This book will definitely begin to develop this skill in you, as your mobility between your four storeys grows more familiar and easy. The knack of being open-hearted, comfortable and safe with emotions is being able to – even in the midst of them – stay clear-minded and aware, watching from your third floor and noticing, 'Gee, I am angry,' or 'Whoa, that is a big wave of sadness going through me.' And also to be open in talking about it with loved ones.

5

SPECIAL SECTION

The Trauma We All Need to Heal

Note: Throughout the course of this book, we are occasionally going to 'break out' of the sequential flow of the chapters and apply what we have learned so far to a real-world problem. This first breakout section tackles one of the most harmful factors to human happiness, peace and cooperation: the astonishing toll taken by intergenerational trauma. The strong evidence emerging that almost everyone in the twenty-first century is wounded by the century that went before – and how to diagnose and heal from that in your own case.

You can skip these sections if you prefer, but I encourage you to stay. This is where 'the rubber hits the road' in terms of using what you have learned so far to make your life take a different and vastly better course.

I don't know if you have friends or family who are in the nursing profession, but they are rather a unique bunch. I married into a family of five nurses, and my social world includes many more.

It tends to make a mere psychotherapist shut up and listen when their intense and life-and death world is briefly opened to view. Once, long ago, sitting round a table late at night, some very senior sisters told me something that made my hair stand on end. *Nurses can see illness in the people around them.* Just walking down the street or at the supermarket, they find themselves, if they are not careful, diagnosing complete strangers and passers-by. It can be a little hard to turn off, and a sign that they perhaps need a holiday!

Psychotherapists see the world differently too. We are trained to notice when people are struggling, in the small signs their faces give, the way they breathe and how they hold their bodies. And, of course, our work involves people confiding things that even their best friends do not know about. So we know something that most people don't – that many people who seem to be doing just fine *are actually not*. In this chapter, we'll look at stunning evidence that unresolved trauma – personal and intergenerational – is so common that it affects the lives of almost everyone. This is reassuring to know if you have found life hard – 'You're not Robinson Crusoe', as my old dad used to say (meaning, 'You're not alone'). It's basically the reason for the mental health crisis being experienced worldwide today. But at least knowing the scale of the problem means we can now roll up our sleeves and do something about it. And put into action the knowledge running through this whole book – that trauma can be healed.

In This Together

In the 1960s, there were two big leaps forward in the counselling world. The first was the advent of group therapy, working on problems together instead of always keeping people apart. And, closely related to that, the upsurge of self-help groups such as Alcoholics Anonymous, and countless others – from breast-cancer survivors to single dads.

These two breakthroughs essentially changed our world. From being a culture that kept everything under wraps (with terrible consequences – incest, alcoholism, family violence, unresolved grief and secret illness), we began emerging into the healing light of day. It's the great joy of therapy groups to see people thaw out of their initial reserve and grow incredibly close as they realize that all of us have struggles, and that's okay. And to begin to heal, sometimes with a rapidity that puts older methods of psychiatry to shame – coming off medications, realizing that often the problem is in the world and not in their heads. Feeling a healing anger instead of a crippling inferiority.

In the decades that followed, this culture of more open sharing has led to a different view of human courage and dignity, one that understands that what makes human beings really shine is not success or perfection, but how brave it is to

open our hearts and keep on growing despite the many
setbacks and harms we have endured. I am in no doubt, dear
reader, that you are on this heroic journey too.

It's a process that still has far to travel. Just look at the basic
facts – the 40-per-cent rate of marriage breakdowns, the seemingly intractable problem of family violence, the recent
epidemic of anxiety in young people, the growing suicide
problem even among prosperous and successful people – all
these shout out to us that something is amiss. If only one in
fifty people had a psychiatric illness, it would be plausible to
blame some brain or chemical imbalance. When the figure is
one in five, or more, then we have to look at another ex-
planation: that the problem is not with our brains, or bodies,
but with the way we live.

In this chapter, we'll show you the compelling evidence that
almost everyone who grows up in an industrial or post-industrial
society is traumatized. Firstly, through 'adverse childhood
experiences' – a way of quantifying harmful incidents or situations that disrupt childhood. And secondly, through even
normal conditions of living in the modern world, which are
so divergent from what our senses, nervous systems, bodies
and brains were designed for. These are big claims, but in the
therapy world they are becoming a strong consensus.

This is not an argument that the past – at least for many
centuries – was a great place to be. Nor that we should reject
the many great advances made in human wellbeing. But that
the last century simply delivered such massive harms – with
catastrophic wars, recessions, refugee flows, social changes to

family, community and our relationships with nature – that we have accumulated a trauma legacy that lives in the bodies of most of us. And our current way of life is making it worse.

This chapter will help to make clear, in your own personal life, what damage you may be carrying, and what to do about it.

Adverse Childhood Experiences

Sometimes the biggest breakthroughs in medicine happen by complete accident. In the 1990s, a large US health insurer called Kaiser Permanente created a national network of weight-loss clinics, to cater to its largely middle-class – and presumably well-upholstered – membership.[4]

Despite strong enrolments at the start, the company were dismayed to find that almost half of participants were dropping out. Kaiser decided to investigate and a study was begun. Those who quit the programme were given anonymous surveys that were comprehensive and in-depth. The researchers each had an open mind, but what they found was deeply shocking. The dropout group had a distinctive common factor – *a very high incidence of being sexually abused in childhood*. This raised two questions: how could such a terrible childhood experience be linked to dangerous levels of weight gain? And a much bigger question: was sexual abuse really this widespread, un-acknowledged and unspoken about in the general population?

In the 1990s, I had come to this conclusion too. I worked

throughout that decade, training psychotherapists in intensive six-month programmes, and we were shocked to find that around a third of our trainees had been sexually abused, and another third had suffered other trauma, such as the death of a sibling, being in a violent or addictive family, a tragic accident and so on. This began to form the belief I still hold, that the best therapists have 'been there' in their own lives and so can help others from this depth of understanding.

Vincent Felitti, Kaiser's lead researcher, knew this had to be properly addressed. He sought help from the Centers for Disease Control and Prevention, which manages epidemics and large-scale health issues in the US. They randomly selected 17,000 members of the health fund; these were people who by definition were financially secure – they were 75 per cent white, and their average age was fifty-seven. Most had graduated college, all had good jobs.

They were given the questionnaire, and then the findings were matched against their health status, to which the health insurer, of course, had detailed access. It was an unprecedented window into things that we don't usually know about the people around us. What they found made medical history and has changed how we view contemporary life forever after. But first, here are the questions.

(Most readers will answer these for themselves, and that is a very useful thing to do. Do be aware of bringing memories to light, and slow down or take a break if you feel unsettled. If you are uncomfortable in an ongoing way, be sure to seek professional help.)

ADVERSE CHILDHOOD EXPERIENCES SCALE

Before you were eighteen years of age . . .

1. Did a parent or other adult in the household often or very often swear at you, insult you, put you down or humiliate you? Or did they act in a way that made you afraid that you might be physically hurt? YES/NO

2. Did a parent or other adult in the household often or very often push, grab, slap or throw something at you? Or did they ever hit you so hard that you had marks or were injured? YES/NO

3. Did an adult or person at least five years older than you ever touch or fondle you or have you touch their body in a sexual way? Or did anyone attempt or actually have oral, anal or vaginal intercourse with you? YES/NO

4. Did you often or very often feel that no one in your family loved you or thought you were important or special? Or did your family not look out for each other, feel close to each other or support each other? YES/NO

5. Did you often or very often feel that you didn't have enough to eat, had to wear dirty clothes and had no one to protect you? Or were your parents too drunk or high to take care of you or take you to the doctor if you needed it? YES/NO

6. Was a biological parent ever lost to you through divorce, abandonment or other reason? YES/NO

7. Was your mother (or stepmother) often or very often pushed, grabbed, slapped or had something thrown at her? Or sometimes, often, or very often, kicked, bitten, hit with a fist or hit with something hard? Or was she ever

repeatedly hit for at least a few minutes or threatened with a gun or knife? YES/NO

8. Did you live with anyone who was a problem drinker or alcoholic, or who used street drugs? YES/NO
9. Was a household member depressed or mentally ill, or did a household member attempt suicide? YES/NO
10. Did a household member go to prison? YES/NO

Your score is simply the total of YES answers.[5]

In short, there are ten factors – emotional abuse, physical abuse, sexual abuse, emotional neglect, physical neglect, divorce or loss of a parent, family violence, parental alcoholism or addiction, mental illness, incarceration. Of course, those ten were only some of the things that could go wrong in a child's formative years, as there was no mention of poverty, war, racism, lack of educational opportunities, poor housing or disease, but the ACE items perhaps sum up the effects of these within a family, which is where children experience them the most intensely.

How Common Trauma Really Is

What astonished the researchers was how very common such trauma was. Felitti's team found that 67 per cent of the sample had at least one ACE point, while 40 per cent had a score of at least two. Over 12 per cent had a score of FOUR OR MORE. Remember, this was a well-off group of people. (As established, only well-off people can afford health insurance in the US, unlike Australia and the UK, where health care is a human right.) For a racial minority, on low incomes, living in substandard conditions (as at least a quarter of American or British people do), the scores would presumably be far, far worse. The Centers for Disease Control and Prevention would later conduct many studies and find that, in the general population, across all income groups, having four or more ACE points occurred in *one person in six*. Have another glance at the list and you will realize that is an awful lot of trauma.

But this wasn't all. Now came the point for which the researchers had been wanting answers. When they cross-checked the health records of the participants, they found that high ACE scores correlated with terrible health. And, they were soon to add, were often the cause of that poor health.

Those with four or more points had *double the rates of heart disease and cancer*, and *four times the risk of lung disease*. A traumatic childhood made people very unwell. In some cases, it was because this kind of childhood led to risky behaviour, like poor nutrition, smoking and drinking, and in turn that affected health. But sometimes these awful childhood experiences brought about actual physical changes to the body, the immune system and the brain, which made people unwell and shortened their lives, often by decades.

By the 2020s, health-care experts such as Dr Nadine Burke Harris were calling for all adults and children to be given the

ACE test, so that their health and treatment could be planned accordingly. Burke Harris and other researchers found indications that the original risk factor – sexual abuse as a child – was so stressful that it altered the metabolism of children, so that problem eating/weight gain/diabetes was a highly likely sequel. To the already complex causes of obesity was added a new factor – that stress caused the body to store fat differently.

The most upsetting fact to emerge was that what is called epigenetic change – alterations to the way our DNA is expressed – could pass on this harm into many generations that follow. It's likely that many so-called mystery diseases – chronic fatigue, fibromyalgia, some autoimmune conditions – may have this kind of epigenetic causation. Burke Harris believes that, until we address making childhood safer and families more secure, we will not be able to solve or eliminate these severe conditions that affect millions of people.

To lighten the gloom of all this, there is a hopeful note. My experience, and that of almost all therapists, is that *some people with high ACE scores still live happy and healthy lives*. The scale does not cover the positives in a child's life, and researchers are clear that help for children at the time of trauma or after can mitigate these harms. For millions of children, having a caring grandparent, an understanding teacher, a staunch and empathic friend can help them to bounce back. One parent in a family might be very damaging, but the other parent is able to counter that. Even years later, we can provide what is now termed 'trauma-informed treatment' to more children and young people and help them get through. It would be better if it never happened, but trauma need not be a life sentence. Our bodies and minds were designed to heal, and we just have to know how to activate those powers.

Why Is There So Much Trauma?

If we zoom right back to the big picture, the ACE scores demand we address a very big question – what the hell has gone wrong with our society? How did we come to have so many damaged and damaging families?

To answer that, we have to remember just what a nightmare the twentieth century was – especially the first half. Over a hundred million killed in two world wars, and another hundred in genocides. The Great Depression, refugee flows in the hundreds of millions, and the overall shift from rural community to urban living, with the nightmare of the Industrial Revolution lying in between. What we see now in East Asia – child workers sleeping beneath their factory tables at night, people dying of preventable diseases in horrendous slums – that was our history too, just a century ago. (The Grenfell Tower disaster showed that it could so easily return.)

Look into your family history and it's unlikely that you escaped this. As I was writing this chapter, I met with an old friend, a kindly and much-respected minister in a peaceful Tasmanian country town. But he was born in London in 1935, and he and his mother were bombed out of their home three times before he was eight years old. His soldier father was absent for five years, then was barely emotionally available ever after.

The surgeon who operated on me when I became unwell a couple of years ago was a Vietnamese 'boat person' who made a nightmare journey to safety at the age of five. Our family dentist fled the Czech uprising as a teenage boy. My neighbour, a warm and caring dad, married to an Australian wife, spent six despairing years in a desert concentration camp as a young man, courtesy of the Australian government. His health was seriously and permanently damaged. You will probably know people who survived conflict in Iraq, Northern Ireland, the Falklands or Afghanistan, or peacekeeping in Kosovo or East Timor. Nobody, it seems, has a remotely straightforward family background. Traumatized people (and that means almost all of us today – see the next box) may not function well as parents or providers. Overwhelmed by stress, they may become violent, withdrawn, abusive, substance abusing or suicidal. If nothing or nobody intervenes, the harms just echo on and on. That is why we simply must intervene.

Because of how widespread such damage is, we have to adjust our settings on how we see our fellow human beings, and quite probably ourselves. We assume that most people, most of the time, have had pretty reasonable lives. (And that poor health, when it does happen, is often just bad luck.) We think of PTSD as being the domain of war veterans, emergency workers or accident survivors. What the ACE studies indicate is that it is part of the mental health picture of almost every second child and adult.

IS NORMAL LIFE TRAUMATIC?

A colleague and friend of mine, David Jockelson, has had an interesting career path. He is a community lawyer with a lifetime of experience with child protection cases, but has also worked for fifteen years as a psychotherapist. He campaigns across the UK for better mental health care for legal professionals, who themselves are an at-risk group.

David has done a great deal of thinking and writing on trauma and normal life. One of his most intriguing ideas is that trauma does more than just cause massive anxiety, it also may act as a brake on our development. Trauma can freeze us at the age when it took place, at least on some dimensions of maturation which require trust, learning and physiological calm to proceed well. As a consequence, we see many adults today who are still emotionally frozen in an infantile stage of development, for example, or an adolescent one. If this is very widespread, then a whole society can become skewed towards certain kinds of immaturity. David believes, and I am inclined to agree, that we have a somewhat adolescent culture today. This manifests in a reduced ability to or interest in caring for others, and a deep obsession with one's own image, status or gratification. An unwillingness to make committed relationships, and so on. That this is connected to trauma is the new ingredient in understanding it. But – what is the trauma that might be responsible?

Recently, he and many other researchers and thinkers have been asking the question: what if our normal living conditions today are so far from what we are designed for, that they simply damage our brains?

Things like . . .

- Increasing use of long daycare for younger and younger children.
- Increasingly pressured nature of school, with intense testing and competition even in the early years.
- Exposure to relentless media in our living spaces at home.
- Long working hours for parents, and the unaffordability of taking time off work just to care for each other.
- Urban environments with little access to nature.
- Very stressed lives leading to relationship collapse and family breakdown becoming almost the norm.

The Adverse Childhood Experiences scale shows widespread harm in normal people, but – and common sense supports this – its ten items may not be the only varieties of trauma there are. Added to this, some children and adults are vastly more sensitive to stimuli, and find modern life an assault on their senses and ability to cope.

UK educator Kim J. Payne wrote a book called *Simplicity Parenting,* which started a whole movement towards drastically reducing activity levels, busyness and clutter from children's and parents' lives. Kim believes that many conditions suffered by children today begin merely as quirks or tendencies, but are exacerbated into full-grown pathologies simply by the pressure of modern childhood.

Could everyday life in cities and towns today be harming our nervous systems, which evolved for much slower, gentler and more nurturing environments? It makes sense that what we were designed for – the presence of nature, rhythms of light and dark, the company of animals, being around plants and working outdoors, using our bodies much more, in solitude and with time to dream – might be essential to mental and physical health, to proper brain development and our ability to build a sense of peace.

What happens to children who just don't have that? If this 'abnormal living' theory were true, we would expect to see signs of it. Like having one in five girls and young women suffering clinical anxiety. Like rising rates of suicide among the young. Like one in four employees in the workplace having mental health problems. All things that we do actually have.

Getting Free

The first thing is clear – a wound has to be tended, like a deer in the forest, resting somewhere shady and licking the wounded place to help it heal. If you (or someone you love) had items on the ACE scale, you have to acknowledge, yes, this has hurt me. That is the first step in healing. So often, people discount those things – 'Yes, I was sexually abused', or 'Yes, Mum drank herself to oblivion', or 'Yes, Dad used to hit Mum', but everything is fine, that's in the past. That may be true, but if you have difficulties now, in the present day, the connection might be worth exploring. If you carry a wounded child inside you, they might need some care.

The 'focusing' methods of Eugene Gendlin that we described

earlier in this book are especially helpful, since, as you listen to your body signals (your supersense), in any time of difficulty, they will lead you to your healing edge. Tears that need to be cried, shudders of fear to be let go of, furious anger that does not belong to now but has been 'triggered' by now and has to find a safe way to come out.

Your body talks to you all the time about these things. A dear friend of mine was often hit by her father as a child. She vowed never ever to hit her kids, or allow anyone else to, and she succeeded. But, on one especially bad day, when her kids were proving impossible, as all little kids do, and she was also stressed and unwell, she suddenly felt an impulse, right through her body, to swing back her hand and belt them. She was self-aware enough to just feel that, notice it, and let it go. She knew what it was and where it came from. Occasionally that urge came back, and each time she let it go she was safer.

PTSD is usually most severe when a person (and this is most of us) does not have access to all four storeys of their mind. Being out of touch with our body is the most common problem, and so we get stuck on the third floor, with repetitive and obsessive thought patterns. Or only some emotions are available on the second floor – fear but not anger, or anger but not sadness. And, of course, we experience isolation from lacking a spiritual place to feel joined to other people, to nature, and to a sense of safety and peace regardless of outer circumstance. When all of our mind is available, we digest and process trauma routinely, and while this still might be dramatic and intense, it does not accumulate.

So, use the four storeys to get through bad moments – notice your body and what it is telling you. Notice your emotions, and let your body be grounded so they can either settle and resolve, or else drive you and energize you to make change. Think, write things down if you need to, or, if you are struggling, talk to someone caring and patient to get your thinking sorted out. And always go to the fourth floor, the rooftop garden, to be reminded that the universe loves you, that you belong and that you are okay. Even just sitting in a park or walking outdoors helps your brain to do this.

Deciphering the Messages

Every person is unique, both in the messages and experiences they received as a child, and in the way they responded to them. The task of therapy is to enlist your supersense to help access these messages and experiences, and then use neuroplasticity to rewire the way you respond if they are no longer helping you. Human beings were made for trauma – prehistoric life was tough – and we have the equipment to grow from it. But unless we were raised (and few of us were) with that equipment fully operational, we get stuck. Therapy's focus should always be on restoring proper functioning. The patient then heals himself (or herself).

In 1980, I won a Churchill Fellowship to train with some of the best-regarded psychotherapy teachers in the world at that

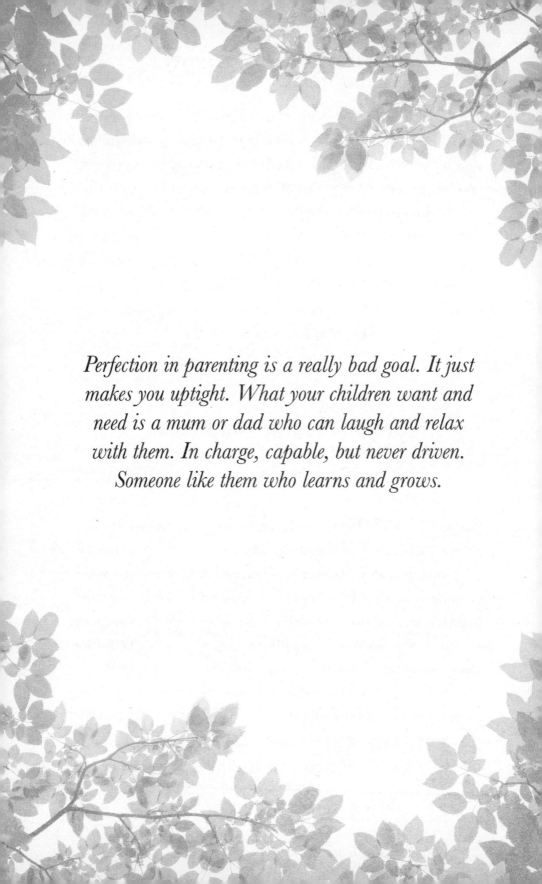

Perfection in parenting is a really bad goal. It just makes you uptight. What your children want and need is a mum or dad who can laugh and relax with them. In charge, capable, but never driven. Someone like them who learns and grows.

time. Robert and Mary Goulding had arrived at a methodology that was shown in outcome studies to have brought the most rapid change, in the most efficient way (group psychotherapy, in intensive short residential programmes). They did this by combining cognitive approaches – clear teaching – with emotional relearning through an approach called Gestalt therapy that involves action and interaction (not just talk). The Gouldings' approach begins with examples of current life difficulties, and from there works to uncover the messages received from early life that have hung around below the level of our awareness, making it hard for us to be happy and fully alive.[6]

The Gouldings trained thousands of therapists in what was called redecision work – how to gently coactivate those old memories of childhood alongside the resources of our mature and understanding selves, so that childhood suffering could be let go of. It was brain surgery without needing to open up your skull.

The Gouldings believed that it was not what was explicitly said to children during childhood that carried the power. In fact, most of our parents said things that were just fine: 'Of course I love you', 'We only want what's best for you.' It was the non-verbal messaging – the struggling child inside each of our parents, who was silently screaming at us through their body language and behaviour. Our supersense told us the true story, and we took it automatically to heart.

If you, dear reader, are a parent of a child or a teenager, you might be feeling quite worried about this idea of transmitted harms that we aren't aware of. Some perspective is important. Firstly, you undoubtedly got more toxic messages, more powerfully transmitted, than your children could ever receive from you. You made it this far, are reading this book, and have made it to adulthood, partnership and parenthood. Your kids can do at least that well. The renowned UK paediatrician and psychoanalyst D. W. Winnicott coined the term 'good enough' parenting and urged us to relax, as that was all kids needed – just to be loved, fed and kept safe as they grew up in the world, and they would find their own way. In my talks, I found another way to express this more humorously: 'the job of parents is to keep you alive until help comes along'. Perfectionism in parenthood is a really bad goal; it just makes you too uptight. What your children want is a mum or dad who can laugh and relax with them, who is human and makes mistakes, and that is okay.

At the same time, one of the things we can do as parents is commit to our own healing. Just as you might drive more carefully, eat more healthily or drink less alcohol because you have children, you also might decide to get counselling or other help, or just at least be honest with yourself that you have struggles in some part of your life that need attention. Caring for yourself is essential for caring for your children.

The Gouldings believed in being simple and practical. They simplified the messages parents send to children, below the level of awareness, to just nine or ten 'injunctions'. They believed that, as children, in order to survive in our families, we 'signed up' to these messages, because at the time that was the wisest thing to do. But these decisions soon become automatic and hard to even recognize. As we grow into adulthood, they operate below the level of conscious awareness, and prevent us from living happy and full lives. If this sounds a bit mystifying, the examples that follow will make it much easier to recognize . . .

THE INJUNCTIONS

Each injunction, or message that parents send to children, begins with a 'Don't', followed by a specific basic human need:

Don't think – this is common when a parent has an addiction, or there is a large family secret not to be questioned. Or it may be role-modelled by parents who are rarely sensible, flapping or agitating instead of working things out one step at a time. Or it can just be, 'Don't think your thoughts; we will tell you what to think' – this often occurs in religious fundamentalist families. With this injunction, you may find you go blank under stress, or get busy in ways that don't help or address the problem at hand. You have to show real determination to relearn – sit down and write problems down, list possible solutions and so on. Or get a counsellor's help specifically to learn to be logical.

Don't be close – this often occurs a generation after sexual abuse. For example, if a mum was abused in her childhood, she might have concluded in her young mind that all touch is dangerous. She is then unable to warmly hold or hug her children. Again, the way through this is to gradually use the four storeys of your mansion to relax and let panic die down when you are hugging or being hugged. Do it gradually, in small steps. (Often some support from a therapist is needed, as abuse has many consequences and strong trust is needed to overcome these.)

Don't feel – this can be specific to one of the four primary emotions, or it can be across the board. Very few people grow up with the full suite of emotions comfortably allowed, and this can continue down many generations. You will know this one is present if you go numb or 'hyperreasonable' when others are upset. Or when a particular emotion seems to be missing from your repertoire – you never get angry, or never get sad. Using your supersense to notice emotions and to gradually 'make room' for them in your body will start to reassure you that the world doesn't end if you use a loud voice or shed a tear. In fact, it feels rather good.

Don't be important – having one-to-one time with Mum or Dad, winning praise for creativity or hard-won achievement, having a fuss made of you on your birthday – all these say, 'You are special.' From these, a child learns to self-value, and feel they have a place in the universe. For some people – often in larger families – for any child to be held in esteem was seen as a kind of affront to everyone else, and so the survival message became that self-erasure was what was most valued. You know you have this when it is incredibly hard to accept praise or be the centre of attention. (When my old mum had her seventieth birthday, we made a huge banner that we put across the front porch of the reception centre where we gathered, for all the world to see. It read: *I Don't Want Any Fuss*. She thought it was wonderful!)

Don't belong – whether superior, or inferior, you are told that 'Our family are different'. Or that you are different and cannot ever feel that lovely sense of being one of the group. You have to hold yourself apart, however lonely and crippling that might be. I had this injunction, though being on the autism spectrum probably didn't help. You just feel like an outsider, it's awfully lonely, and it's important to find your 'tribe' and learn to join in.

Don't grow up – often a child can fill a role in the life of a parent that holds that parent together or removes the need for that parent to venture out into the world. For example, a lonely or even narcissistic mother might want their daughter or son to always be their friend, their emotional comfort. Or they may have an unresponsive partner and look to a child for companionship. Or, unconsciously, this child might be planned to be their old-age support person. Others in the family are excused this role, but the favourite is rewarded and prioritized, since they will be asked to repay in full when the time comes.

(One of my patients remembers falling in love with a girl and going to visit her at home. Her mother sat with them the entire time he was there and took issue with his views on almost everything they discussed. Even as a dopey teenage boy, he told me, he could not miss the blatant gatekeeping. The daughter remained single and devoted to her mother for the rest of her life.)

Don't be a child – the overresponsible child, who is like a little adult, is another very common family role. Perhaps through alcoholism or addiction, or mental health problems in a parent, there was no time to be little and play and enjoy themselves, so growing up fast was required. The child took care of the adults. It was something that an elder child, or a female child, was often recruited into, consciously or unconsciously. Once this role was filled, sometimes other children were let off the hook, but if the parental dysfunction was severe, a whole tribe of children might team up to take care of Mum or Dad. You know you've got this injunction if you just can't be silly or horse around. You spend your days off cleaning and don't do fun things. In our therapy groups, we would set homework to be lazy, let other people be kind to you, play frisbee during the breaks. Having a dog can help, too.

Don't succeed – success is really a feeling, rather than an actual benchmark, and many people in childhood experi-ence being 'never good enough'. That simple stupidity of asking a child who gets 98 per cent what went wrong with the other 2 per cent. To overcome this, it's important to realize that it's a choice. You already are successful, but you just need to notice that, and learn to bask in it. People who love you can help by pointing this out. It seems to help to picture the parent or parents who gave this message, and tell them to fuck off!

Don't be you – this often relates to the gender you are. A family wanted a son (at least unconsciously) and got daugh-ters, or vice versa. It can also relate to children who begin to show signs of being LGBTQ+. The family simply wants something else. But it can also just relate to being artistic or athletic when they wanted an intellectual. Or to any number of unconscious obsessions being loaded onto a child. The net effect is a feeling that you cannot just be you – a terrible thing to feel. Again, tell your parents calmly and resolutely – in real life or in your imagination – I am me! I am going to be me! It's not my problem that you wanted something else. Then find caring people who like you as you are, surrogate parents who affirm the real you.

Don't be well – in all the injunctions, the message is reinforced by what, in our early childhood, got us attention. Unless children get 'strokes' through being noticed, cared for, praised and cuddled, they fail to thrive. Connection and affirmation are so important that children will do anything to get 'attention' – even if it's negative attention. Sometimes a family does not know how to care or show affection or attention, except when a child is sick. This redefines it as medical, and being cared for – even very minimally – may be the only attention a child ever gets. Not all poor health is a choice, but overwork, risk-taking, or other actions can produce it, and this can become a lifetime 'script'.

Always remember, the injunctions are not spoken or even intended messages, but are conveyed by the deeper feelings and struggles of parents – non-verbally, for the most part. This is where their power lies, and why it takes some care to uncover them. Nobody normally intends to put these constraints onto the children they love.

The help that understanding the injunctions brings is that you can *connect the trauma in your childhood to the specific way it is impacting you now*. For example . . .

'Dad used to get violent when he was drunk, and the way I adapted was to freeze and make my mind a blank (don't think). That was smart of me then, but it doesn't help when my kids are being naughty now.'

'Mum died when I was nine and Dad just fell to pieces. I had to look after my younger brothers and sisters, and him as well (don't be a child). I was a brave kid, but now I need to learn to relax.'

Figuring out which injunctions you took on means that suddenly your life can make sense, but more than that, you then know what to attend to, which 'wounds to lick', so they can heal. Understanding is the start, but exploring your awareness of this in the present is what makes it all come together. A good therapist can help this go a lot faster, but, just using your Four-Storey Mansion, you can bring yourself more and more into the present to be free. You begin to notice the times you feel like a little child, and by staying with the body sensations, listening closely to your supersense, you progressively let these dissolve. In the healing phase, you will have the sense of the past still being activated in you, alongside knowing that it was the past and is not the case today. Soon, it will be less and less of a problem, you will feel stronger and at peace.

Figuring Out Your Injunctions

If you want to grow without a therapist's help, the first step is to look at whatever current difficulty you are having, and which injunction might be at play. You know you are up against an 'out of awarenes' injunction when you repeatedly have the same kind of problem – choosing the same kind of toxic partner, losing jobs in the same way, having the same kind of 'accident' or, hopefully, less dramatic occurrences – never belonging, never feeling worthwhile: whenever something begins to look awfully like a pattern, a theme that repeats.

So, it helps to ask yourself, What conditions in my childhood made this an adaptive behaviour at the time? (Even low self-esteem is a way of coping with an unsupportive family.) Healing starts with first appreciating your smart self, at that age, for finding a survival strategy, and then deciding that it's time for a different way of life, because you are no longer a child and no longer dependent on the crazy kind of family you grew up in. (That almost all of us twentieth-century children grew up in.)

Childhood decisions, now out of awareness, have a characteristic pattern: they feel like a cling-wrap wall, holding us back from living a full life that others seem to be having. We can't see the wall, but we keep bouncing back off it.

Most people find that, on reading the list, one or two of the injunctions 'light up in neon', and seeing that is the first step to unwiring that programming. Most of us have at least two or three injunctions, and generally the one you notice is one that has already begun to resolve. Once that is done, others more deeply buried may begin to surface. But, at every step, your life will be freer and more joyful.

There have been many tough times in history – wars, genocides, famines and pandemics are not new. But the twentieth century had them all, and on a planetary scale, with little time to recover before the next hammer blow fell. I can still see the echoes of my grandfather's war in the trenches, on my father's struggles, and my mother's anxieties, and so into my own. It wasn't anybody's fault. Your parents and mine were most likely doing their very best.

As long as you are alive, your mind will continue on a healing path, through dreams, thoughts and memories surfacing as they are ready to be resolved. Using your supersense to let them move through you (not numbing or blocking them, but slowing down to give them your full attention) while staying strongly grounded in the present, you cannot fail to become more whole and more at peace.

We came into a world of damaged parents and families, and some of that surrounded us as we grew up. We adapted to that at the time, in the very best way to ensure survival. But pinpointing and releasing those self-limitations prevents them becoming a lasting harm – and means we never need to put those onto our own children, partners or friends. That alone is a very good reason to get well.

Much love to you as you travel this journey home. It's a journey we are all on.

6

THE THIRD FLOOR

Using Your Brain to 'Think Straight'

The third floor of our Four-Storey Mansion, technically speaking, is our 'prefrontal cortex', the place where we do our thinking. It's where you are right now, reading this book. It may seem a familiar place, but there is more to this floor than meets the eye – hazards to watch out for, and also whole new rooms you haven't looked in, with great views out the windows and lovely furniture!

Our thinking brains are amazing; with them, we created hospitals, invented spaceships and little devices on which we can talk to friends on the other side of the Earth. With all this power, you would think we would have built a happy, balanced and, above all, durable world. So, you have to ask – why are we in such a mess? Perhaps we haven't used our brains all that well, after all. In this chapter, we'll help you get your head together with the rest of you, so that it actually works as it was designed to. Let's start with a story . . .

The acclaimed Scots mountaineer and writer Andrew Greig had suffered from depression and struggled with self-doubt all through his teens and early adult years. But he discovered something that saved his life – that wild places and physical effort out in nature seemed to help him find peace. Like most young people, he was also exploring intimacy and relationships, and finding them hard to navigate . . .

My ex-lover had been away on a long adventure, not found what she was looking for, and come back single again. We talked for a time then sat near each other among the long grass above the reservoir. When she had finished her story of that man, those places, she glanced at me.

'So it's full circle,' she said.

I knew what was being offered. I breathed in the thin air of the moorland hills, felt the solid ground below, and the open sky above.

'I love you,' I said. Part of me waited, appalled. 'But I don't want you.'

And in the saying, it was true. She looked out over the hills and choppy water, wind shifting her sun-bleached hair. She glanced at me, then nodded.

'Yes,' she said. 'Do you think I've something wrong with my heart?'

We walked back to the city, went our ways, and never met on that ground again. Had it happened indoors we might have been confused by our bodies, our loneliness, our losses, but out among the hills and water, we said and did right.

At the Loch of the Green Corrie *(Quercus, 2010)*

Listen again to that pivotal sentence . . . '*And in the saying, it was true.*' So often, that is how we find our truth. We search to put into words what has been in our hearts, and it's only when we say them out loud that we know they ring true. And notice that she says, 'Yes.' She knows it too.

This was a woman to whom he had given his heart, and she had left him, for larger adventures, and for another man. And now here she was. Instinctively, he knows what to do. He grounds himself in the landscape. He listens to his own insides and what they are telling him. Then, the precision of language is carefully wielded. 'I love you' – spoken with compassion. 'But I don't want you.'

This is one of the clearest, and most beautifully written, instances I've ever read of using every level – body, heart and brain – and using our supersense, the inner signals from our body, to find integrity and avoid disaster.

Often in life we do not know what to do. We may default to relying on rules, or codes of behaviour, and this is a whole lot better than not giving a damn. Sometimes the rules are right: Don't sleep with someone else's wife or husband. Don't drink and drive. Don't do needless harm. But, in some things, what is truly moral is more complex. Deep inside us, the truth is there, and it has subtleties that no rule book could ever handle. Feel 'the solid ground below, and the open sky above', as Greig so clearly writes. Wait, and it will come. It will come in words. And the words will 'make sense.'

The Floor Where Words Live

The third floor of our mansion is the latest 'addition' in evolutionary terms, which is why it's located at the very front of our brain – like a new extension on a house. Animals can think, but only in smells, pictures, muscle memory and the like. There are birds that use tools, and even make tools (they sharpen bits of wood for digging out grubs), which shows planning and some interesting levels of intelligence. But the addition of words takes it to a whole new level. Words can travel, and they can last. Words can build a bridge of understanding between people. They also allow for extraordinary subtlety. The Japanese have a word just for the feeling when you discover a waterfall in a forest: *yugen*. German has a word for enjoying pompous people's misfortune: *schadenfreude*. We import words for things we didn't previously have or need. Like *joie de vivre* or 'hassle'!

The first use of language was practical. The mammoth is coming! Stand your ground! Run! Soon our species fell in love with words and talked endlessly as they trailed along riverbanks all day, or sat around campfires at night. The ancient world had thousands of unique languages, a different one in each valley. And since most peoples interacted with neighbouring language groups, it was normal for humans to speak two or three distinct tongues. Our brains grew larger in order to handle the need for and the joy of, words.

We do two things with words, both hugely important. First, we use them to make sense of our own life. To make our actions rational, logical. And second, we communicate our inner worlds and ideas to each other, so we can coordinate and have a happy time.

Our thinking is not, as we have been led to believe, an isolated kind of thing, not dry or removed from the rest of us. After all, the term 'making sense' did not arise by chance; it seems to say that our senses are the test – something is only right when confirmed by direct experience. We all know people who spin off, ungrounded, into the most arcane and arid places, who can 'bore for England'. The social sciences, which should nurture and help the world we live in, seem especially prone to this. Thinking is at its most brilliant when it taps into its roots in body and heart. This book comes from my third floor, and it reaches out to yours. But if it's to make sense, it will smell good and ring true, and shine light into every floor in your mansion as well.

Thinking Straight

Without language, and the clarity and precision it brings, it is close to impossible to function as a human being. Clarity and straight talk are essential to any relationship. After our love, the ability to think and talk honestly is the most precious skill that parents can give their children. It's what counsellors and therapists help their clients to do, and workers with violent offenders. It's not about fancy language – some of the clearest people I know barely finished primary school. It's about knowing lies from truth. Men's movement leader Robert Bly recommends writing a journal paragraph, or a poem, every day of your life. His reasons are many, but the best is the way it makes you more honest with yourself: 'it's easier to spot a lie when it's written down.'

Many people barely think at all. Nothing interposes between impulse and action beyond a few self-justifying clichés. They have not been given the tools to do so, and their lives are disastrous as a result. When New Zealand prison superintendent Celia Lashlie talked to the men in her 'care', she found that they often had terrible difficulty thinking things through at any time at all, but especially while under pressure. They were in prison, sometimes for a very long time, because they had made a bad choice that took about three minutes; they were unable to think, Is this a good idea? What will be the consequence? Without that ability, in a stressful and complicated world, you are pretty much doomed. When we read stories to children, and talk to them as we go through our day, when we draw out of our teenagers what their thinking is, and listen deeply to them, we are nurturing this power.

How We Learn to Think

As little children, we are all sensation and feeling. We live our days in a timeless dream of cuddles and sleep, food and play. One minute laughter, then tears, now bright lights, then soothing darkness. It's all now. We live on the first two floors of our mansions, and we are content. But a baby or todder also has times of intense frustration – If I could just get them to understand! Luckily, help is on the way.

Let's say we are two years old. We see a brightly coloured teddy bear in a shop window, and we want it. Our mummy isn't buying it, so we cry out in pain and distress. This is not an attempt (as some twentieth-century parenting experts taught) to manipulate or control; it's actual distress. At one or two years of age, we can't cope with the fact that we have these huge urges and wants, and the world is quite indifferent to them.

If we are lucky, our mother understands this. She picks us up and croons softly into the side of our face. 'Yes, I under-stand, you're sad that you can't have that teddy bear. It's okay, it's okay to be sad.' We are furious now. *'I wan' it!'* But she is unfazed. 'It's upsetting to not get what you want', she says. 'Here, let's sit down on this bench.' And she holds you, and you gaze about, figuring out whether to continue or stop. For a time there, the feeling was inescapable; it had to be allowed to run its course. Now, you are not so sure. Some deep grief was there, but it is passing. Her hands are warm, her eyes look understandingly into yours.

You are learning to emerge out of emotion, to weather these internal storms, and at the same time, as part of that, to think. These urges and intensities have names: Want. Hurt. Happy. Dog. Cat. Grandma. Do you want some more to eat? You discover that words are handles on the world. And that, even if we are not the centre of the universe, we can still be happy in the world.

It's all about getting along. About interdependence. Words, along with more ancient languages like touch and glance, are a superb medium for collaboration in the human race.

A friend of mine was babysitting her three-year-old grand-daughter overnight. The little girl wandered into her bedroom early in the morning. She said, 'My body wants to come into your bed.' The speed at which language – and therefore thinking – develops in a child is astonishing, and it delights everyone who is around a growing toddler or young child. They have the freshness of perception, but now can tell us about it, and so give us insights into their world while it is new and intense. This summer, I was teaching a four-year-old child to ride a boogie board in the shallows at the beach, and she was entirely able to use words to make this collaboration work for us both. She could explain to me, 'The big waves are too scary', and I let her just sit on the board in an inch or two of water. In less than a minute, she was saying, 'Take me out again.' I could tell her, 'Sit in the middle of the board to balance,' and she knew what that meant, and immediately put it into prac-tice every time after. I launched her shorewards on a promising wave, she rode it in, and to our surprise the receding wave pulled her back to me so we could do it all again. She laughed aloud and said, 'That wave pulled me conveniently!'

A toddler who is lucky enough to have parents who are not too busy will chatter to them and they will chatter back – it's very rewarding because, above all else, human beings love to connect. Before long, it's stories made up by your dad with funny voices, or people reading books to you at bedtime, and after a year or two you can actually read yourself, and off you go. You are on the third floor of your mansion, well and truly. With words, you can manage life. Words join you to the human race – whether talking with caring friends, or just reading novels or wisdom books. Someone, somewhere has gone through what you are going through. Everyone who cared enough to write something down over the centuries is now part of your care and development. It's really rather awesome to contemplate. This is what language – and thinking – can do.

THREE WAYS TO BE

The best psychology is not always the newest. Wise and observant people have been thinking about human life for a very long time. The following idea of 'three ways to be' is about three thousand years old; it's one of the most powerful self-help tools I've come across, and I use it all the time. It's especially good if you are a person prone to agitation.

Ancient Vedic scriptures describe three states of mind, which you will quickly recognize.

Their Sanskrit (ancient Indian) names are Tamasic, Rajasic and Sattvic. An approximate translation would be:

Tamasic equals *chaotic*
Rajasic means *driven*
Sattvic indicates *harmonized*

I'd encourage you, though, to use the Indian terms, so they lodge in your mind as a new form of self-awareness. So you can say, 'Oh crap, I am totally Tamasic this morning.' By *noticing what state you are in*, you automatically have more choice. But which one is best to choose? Let's explore.

What Tamasic Means

Everyone knows someone – friend or family member – who is chaotic. If you have teenagers in your house, there may be one or two! Their room (or their whole house) is a mess, their life is disorganized. It is full of panic and confusion, alternating with apathy and torpor. Think of a former US president on Twitter, and you get the idea. We're all like this sometimes – we eat mindlessly straight from the fridge, flick aimlessly through channels on TV, fall asleep on the couch, wake in the middle of the night. It can be your usual state, or something that suddenly comes over you, perhaps in a time of grief or deep worry. When it happens, it feels like a swamp you are stuck in. Some people reading this were raised by a parent like this. Perhaps alcohol or drugs played a role, but, whatever the cause, it is hell to be around, and hell to be in, really.

We might be judgmental of a person who is Tamasic, but my experience is that it often arises from a surprising source – it happens most when you are actually very *anxious*. Just because a person looks apathetic or unmotivated, don't assume it's laziness. (Laziness is rarely a natural state in humans, we are naturally creative and active creatures, so it is often a sign of some kind of deep discouragement or anxiety that immobilizes action.) It can at times be a defensive or protective reaction to the world being just too much to face. Procrastinating is Tamasic; fearful of failure, we cast about doing everything but what we need to do. Your actions are running from what you know, deep down, that you need to focus on. The Internet, needless to say, is a very Tamasic place, and can scatter your brain like nothing else on Earth. So, the way out of a Tamasic state is nearly always to calm down, stop doing anything at all, and get to the bottom of what is making you anxious.

When I notice I am getting Tamasic in a big way, I sit down and write about being stuck or unsure what to do next. Isolated inside our minds, our thoughts can go in circles and it can all seem too much, so even a list on a page helps to sort it out. Asterisk what is most important, and do that.

But also, try to work out what is making you anxious. Get to the root, rather than harassing yourself for being useless. You are not useless. Ask your supersense what is going on.

If I am downright anxious, if I can feel that fluttery sense in the area of my heart, I will go for a walk or do some gardening. What is most important is what you don't do. *Don't do things that are numbing* (drinking, eating, binge-watching TV, or gambling) at these times, as those will just land you back where you started once they are over.

It might be that you have to 'feel the fear' and do it anyway. Perhaps you have a worrying health issue, or concerns with finances, or a work issue, but you've done all you can and just need to press on. Sometimes, you are just overwhelmed by how much you have to do. When I can't face the tidying up, I start in literally one corner of my room or our house and work around the walls! Do *something* and it will get you feeling better again.

The Rajasic State of Mind

Rajasic is the opposite of Tamasic – it's a state of being highly, almost obsessively, focused. We've all known someone like this, almost hyperactive in pursuit of their goal. They work obsessively and for long hours into the night, in order to get rich, or to become famous, seduce women, or build a big house or a mighty career. They don't lack organization or purpose. They are single-minded, energized and intense. They might do this for ten or twenty years. The goal might be a good one or a bad one, but the method is the same. A Rajasic person is driven to achieve.

In Western thinking, we often admire this way of going about life, and elevate the great athlete, business person or celebrity. The go-getter is an admired type in our culture. But often, in practice and close up, our supersense feels uneasy around someone like this. It's as if their life has become deeply imbalanced and other aspects of their life are being neglected. They often ride roughshod over others, and their relationships are poor and do not last. If we follow their biography, sooner or later their life comes crashing down.

We've often absorbed a two-choice idea of life, and this is

*Sattvic activity often looks like 'not a lot going on.'
A war is not started . . . a husband and wife
back away from a hurtful escalation . . . a family
discussion is held quietly, with some laughter,
and a surprising new direction is taken.*

always something to be wary of. Faced with a dilemma, it's interesting to see if there is a third way. Lazy or hard-working sounds like it covers all the options, but wait – there's more!

Moving to Sattvic

In the Vedic system, the highest state of mind and way of going about life is called Sattvic. (It's the same root word as in bodhisattva, so, pretty good!) In a Sattvic state, you are still focused and productive, but your actions are no longer 'driven' – they are harmonized, balanced and peaceful. You 'muck in' with other people and their needs and goals, too, so that you aren't like a 'bull in a china shop' (as my old mum used to say). In a Sattvic state, there is a paradoxical feeling of content-ment with the process, as if on some level you have already arrived at the goal you are working towards. Martin Luther King and Gandhi had that as their secret, and I think Angela Merkel and Jacinda Ardern have it too. There may be mighty work to be done, but you are peaceful, deep down, as you go about it. As spiritual teacher Ram Dass once said about his work with death and dying: it's so heavy, it's light. This kind of attitude means you are vastly more effective, not creating a backlash. You are open to new ideas and always adapting to the way that is right to go. You don't crash through things.

Many people move from Rajasic on to Sattvic as they grow wiser about life. In Hermann Hesse's classic novel *Siddhartha*, the young man works tirelessly to earn a fortune and impress a beautiful courtesan. And he succeeds, but it feels empty to him. He leaves it all behind to find a better path. A number of billionaires I have known as friends have made this shift – a singular early focus on wealth turns to, 'How can I help the world?' Their joy in living soared, making their less generous peers look like the sad losers they are.

A martial arts example is aikido – which aims never to hurt another person, but simply redirects their aggression to end in a harmless, even friendly way. A famous aikido master once encountered a huge crazy man on a train, who was terrifying the passengers. He did not, though, use his aikido. He gently asked the man to sit with him, and within a minute, the man was sobbing; his mother had died that morning. The aikido master just sat with an arm around him, and quietly the fellow passengers returned to their seats too.

Sattvic activity often looks like not a lot is going on. But what goes on can be world-changing. It's that tiny pivot point, like an acupuncture needle, that redirects huge energies. A war is not started. A husband and wife back away from a hurtful escalation and forgive each other. A family discussion is held quietly, with some laughter, and a surprising new direction is taken.

So those are the three states, and you are always in one of them. Some spend their entire life in one of the first two, but most of us shift in and out of all three states, many times in a single day. Once you start to identify which state you are in, then even without trying (in fact, not trying is often the best way) you will begin to simply want to move to a better state. Being aware of the states in yourself is all you need to do to begin having more choice and freedom.

And, just for those who like some neuroscience, it turns out that, using an EEG machine to measure brain waves, there are three primary types of brain activity. Theta, Beta and Alpha waves correspond rather well to being Tamasic, Rajasic and Sattvic. But you can tell, you really can, just by the way you feel. Sattvic is like velvet, the world is smooth. You just want to be there all the time.

Sounding Good Doesn't Make it True

Not all thinking is sound or good. Just because some words can make you feel good doesn't make them true. Very early in my career, I helped send a child rapist to prison. He was the de facto partner of the mother of a twelve-year-old girl. When the police arrived at their house, he knew the game was up. Gathering his things to go with them, perhaps conscious of their cold gaze on him, he muttered, 'Someone was going to do it.' And then, in case that wasn't clear enough, 'Best for her that it was someone she knew'.

I've never met a person who has done awful things, that didn't have a story that made it okay in their own mind. We call this 'rationalization'. There's a lot of it around. In my country of Australia, politicians detain small children and families in tropical hellholes offshore, because it wins the votes of frightened folk who have never even met a refugee. They have a story to make this okay: it's being done 'to save lives'. Nobody with half a brain is fooled by this. 'Stopping the boats' really means 'Die somewhere else', but they never say that. There is what you want, and there is what makes it sound okay. And there is what is actually right. On the island of Tasmania where I live, people who want to destroy forests, or mine coal for a quick buck say it's because they want to create jobs. Then they replace their workforces with huge machines. But it's inside our own heads that we need to watch out for this. It can poison a family, and cause enormous stress in children, if we are not honest about our reasons or up front with our needs. We say one thing, but their supersense is telling them – 'That's not true.' Sorting this out really matters.

It's not easy to live with integrity, but a commitment to try to do so will mean you become, over time, someone who can walk with their head high. Often, my favourite part in a book or movie is when a character, generally either a youngster or an old, rheumy-eyed woman or man, suddenly speaks with absolute clarity. The truth, ultimately, is always your friend.

In the 1990s, when my book *Manhood* was first published, it prompted hundreds of men's groups to start up, for men to find mutual support and live better lives. Some of these groups have lasted for twenty years or more, which in our busy times would suggest they became fairly important in those men's lives. Central to the ethos of a men's group is to have a different kind of conversation than might be possible in a pub or changing room. The rule is always to speak from the heart, and when someone does speak, not to advise, or theorize, but simply hear each of them out. Unless we are invited – by caring but straight-talking friends – to make sense of our lives, then very often our lives make little sense. Whenever I read about terrible actions by men – self-harming, or harming others – I feel a pang of grief, because that could have been prevented by a good men's group. I have seen it done many, many times.

In men's groups, or in a therapy group, the calling out of the lie of rationalization is very important. A man talks for five minutes about his marriage troubles, before one of his mates quietly asks, 'Dave, is this really about sex?'

Most people, shockingly, are barely able to think beyond a babble of self-talk with no tie-in to reality. Read the chatter on social media, among many diverse demographics, and you will see that what passes for thinking is often just a collection of recycled clichés. A large proportion of the human race don't actually reason out their lives; they do what they feel like and only go up to the third floor to find a plausible story to make it sound all right in their heads.

School should perhaps include, as a subject around Year 9, an intensive training in how to argue, reason and logically separate fact from feeling. This kind of tough love is the key role of mentoring and parenthood at certain ages. To call our kids out – gently, but with real resolve. Perhaps 80 per cent of parenting is discussion about what makes sense, how things work. Aunties do this well for teenage daughters. They can have long, thoughtful conversations about things too embarrassing to talk to Mum about – 'Sure, he's easy on the eye, but how bored do you wanna be in this life?' They ask questions like, 'What do you want out of life?', 'What would you never put up with?', 'What's the most important thing in life, to you?' They can even call you out – 'You say you want this, but you are doing that.' If nobody flexes these kind of muscles for us, how can they ever grow strong?

The key to understanding the human brain is to understand that it was never designed to function alone. We need to be part of a network of minds, in order to cross-reference and apply some sanity checks. Preferably with people who don't see it our way at all. You can be very fruitfully married to someone with an entirely different world view.

Going Higher

From the basics of thought – shouting at our fellow cave-person not to let the mammoth steaks burn – to organizing ten thousand people for a good cause – we rise higher and higher, eventually to figuring out life itself.

Richard Rohr, the rebel Franciscan priest and a profound thinker about life and purpose, is very good at taking things to this level. Rohr was aware that many adults go through life still thinking like children, and that this has taken our world to a rather dire place. If you and your loved ones, or the world you treasure, is harmed or even destroyed, it's likely to be by little boys (or girls) in large bodies, wielding power that they really should not be trusted with. Politicians, oligarchs, amoral people with vast financial interests, dictators, down to common or garden louts and lost souls – all make our world fraught and unsafe. As we found out in the Covid crisis, they cost a lot of lives.

Rohr set out five understandings – or realizations – that mark the difference between an adult and child. He designed them to be part of a rite of passage, like sacred truths entrusted to young people passing from childhood to adulthood. Here they are . . .

1. You are going to die.
2. Life is hard.
3. You are not that important.
4. Your life is not about you.
5. You can never control the outcomes.

At first glance, these do not exactly land like joyful messages of liberation! It's an Anthony Robbins seminar turned on its head. But stay with them, and your thinking starts to gain a kind of gritty traction on life.

Knowing you will die is important, not only to make you more careful in cars, but also to prevent you wasting your life by numbing it out, or frittering it away in trivia or distraction, needless anxiety or failing to follow your dreams. In his book *Journey to Ixtlan*, Carlos Castaneda's Navajo mentor told him to keep death always by his side, just over his left shoulder, a spur to always walk a 'path with heart'. The knowledge of death has a very life-affirming role, it intensifies our living. One day, it will be game over. Don't waste a moment.

Knowing that life is hard means you are forewarned that nothing worthwhile comes without sometimes crushing effort. That, in a lifetime, there is grief in equal measure to joy, but that it's still worthwhile. (Fred Rogers, mentioned earlier, taught this so sensitively in his programmes for even the tiniest children. He never shied away from sickness, disability and death as real things in children's lives that they needed us to be honest about. Life is hard, but you never have to face it alone; the love of other people is what makes it possible to feel safe and get back on your feet.)

Realizing your ordinariness does not take away your uniqueness, it just imposes a needed humility. It's odd that in the most dehumanizing, conformist culture there has ever been on Earth (especially for teens), we are seduced with messages of our specialness. Selfies, anyone? We matter, profoundly, since we are part of the chain of life and can both protect it and add to it. But we do this best by humbly looking for those gaps where we can take our part, appreciating all the efforts of others that have made our life possible.

Rohr's fifth point is probably the most chastening of all, and so very important to come to terms with – we spend most of our lives learning it. In a marriage, for example, or any lasting relationship, we have a very hard thing to learn: that we must abandon control, if we are to have any intimacy, trust or fun.

In fact, to even choose where to go for dinner! Love is literally a dance, and in a dance you make your moves but you don't treat the other like a shop mannequin; you feel your way with them and hopefully your moves all combine. Millions of men and women do not understand this, and seek to control the other person, fearing that, if they do not, then they will never get their needs met. Sexuality and desire is a huge test of this; we rarely have the same intensity of need at the same time. But a dancing partner is willing to swing and sway and find the rhythm and, above all, treat the other person as an equal, autonomous being. And trust that the music will bring you together.

There is an important distinction here. Our lack of power doesn't mean we should give up on trying to make things the best that they can be. It's one of those paradoxes that reality often involves. Perhaps the greatest is that terrible things like illness, accident, let alone war or disaster, have always been part of human existence.

As a therapist, my whole effort is helping people gain more control of their lives, and as a struggling human being, how to manage my own. But the bottom line is that, while we can steer our little boats, and paddle hard at key moments, storms and whirlpools happen.

Whatever you do, unpredictable forces will sometimes impact on you, sometimes devastatingly. You have two choices – you can live in terror of this, or, in an odd way, relax. It's out of your hands. We can do a great deal to make life safe, healthy and happy, but then we just have to trust. And when awful things happen, remember that we have tools for handling these awful things, because human beings are designed for that.

The Four-Storey Mansion means you don't have to get crushed by life. As psychoanalyst Clarissa Pinkola Estés wrote so beautifully, 'We were made for these times.'

Being Grown Up

Adulthood, then, is a community of those who have realized that life is about living for each other (and the life we are part of). Anything else is a sad travesty, and no real fun at all. The winners in this world are not who you would think, and they rarely make the headlines.

Adulthood does not come with the passage of a certain number of years; there are millions of babies walking around in grown-up bodies, often in positions of great power, and they make our world a dangerous and damaged place. It takes intervention to help us step into adulthood. Those interventions exist in every indigenous culture on earth – they are called rites of passage. Rites of passage have clearly delineated steps, and perhaps the most important is a ritual process for the dying of our old self, so that we can be born in a new place. This is not easy. We can only learn these things in relationships with people who concretely care about us and are in our lives for the long haul – like the elders of a hunter-gatherer tribe, who loved us and would always be there for us in all the stages and hardships of our life. Adulthood for our ancestors did not mean going out into a big, heartless world, but into a caring community of adults, who shared those life-affirming goals. Initiation is how community is built. And so, dear reader, if your life is just too hard, community is where you have to go to find help. Even imperfect help. Everyone, like you, is just finding their way. You should never feel alone.

The ultimate message of Rohr's teaching, of becoming a true adult, is that, having spent twenty years or so achieving independence and a solid sense of self, we then have to throw that away. We 'die to self'. The mature human loves life and its many pleasures, but they know that's not where deep joy is found. They begin more and more to care about and devote themselves to the wellbeing of the people and the life that surrounds them. They take on stewardship of the Earth and give their life – sometimes literally – to that end.

Among my colleagues and friends worldwide, there now is a concerted effort around slowing and reversing the climate emergency, a race which is literally life and death. Projections of a superheated world are that it might only feed and be safe for a billion people in total by the end of this century (in the lifetime of children being born today). Currently we have eight billion. I have had friends – respectable, thoughtful, contributing folks in their sixties and seventies – blockading banks or city streets or MPs' offices, getting arrested, showing up in court, going back and doing it all again. All over the world, elderly, thoughtful, caring people are trying to find safe, peaceful ways to stop the extinction of the human race.

Their own lives are not as precious to them as the knowledge that their grandchildren will have their time in the sun.

So, this is the truly awesome world available on your third floor. You can arrive at a life full of meaning by *consciously deciding to care*. Thinking at its best can ease your suffering, give you a perspective and instil meaning in the tough corners of life. It can transform us from victimhood to mastery of life itself. It's this floor that delineates our species and its potential. We are a meta-creature, and we are going somewhere every bit as exciting as the exploration of outer space.

And it doesn't stop there. Thinking leads upwards to values. Values lead upwards to actions of a very special kind. And then, there is more. One day, exploring your third floor, you come across something very strange. It's a dusty neglected stairway, leading upwards to a trapdoor overhead. As you venture up those stairs, you can hear snatches of music and see light coming from the cracks. What is up there? Before we find out, dear reader, you should pause and gather yourself. Have a break, a cup of tea, and then on we go.

YOUR THINKING BRAIN REFLECTION EXERCISES ONE TO FIVE

Reasoning out your life and choices, and doing it calmly and well, is both a learned skill and something you choose to do, or not.

1. When you were a child, did your parents and family sit and calmly talk things over, and use logic and reasoning to work out the best way to do things?

2. Can you recognize in yourself a tendency to first decide what you want, and then make up reasons to justify it? To yourself? To other people? How willing would you be to give that up?

3. Have you experienced going into an argument and then realizing that the other person is actually right, or even just right from their point of view? Are you able to let a viewpoint drop in the face of evidence to the contrary? Or are you someone who digs in?

4. Which of Richard Rohr's five truths do you most struggle with in your life right now?

   1. You are going to die.

   2. Life is hard.

   3. You are not that important.

   4. Your life is not about you.

   5. You can never control the outcomes.

5. Were there one or two of these that you once would have struggled with, but are now okay about?

TAMING THE CROWD IN YOUR HEAD

One of the most startling findings of modern brain research, and also a strong teaching of the old meditation traditions, is that the self, the us or me that we usually think of, does not actually exist. Put very bluntly, there is no you. Neuroscience has searched long and low for where in your body or brain the actual seat of you-ness might be, and it's just not there. We experience life as a flow, and a continuity, and that helps us put on our shoes and remember to brush our teeth. But we are more like an ocean wave than a brick. We have continuity, but we change all the time. There are many ramifications of this, but one is to realize that 'false selves' can easily take charge and you can be hijacked by entities – parts of your own make-up – which are not really up to the job of your best interests. People with certain brain disorders know the terrifying experience of hearing voices, often judgmental or disturbing ones, harassing or tormenting them, but all human beings have this to a degree – we argue with ourselves or fight against urges or impulses that would do us harm. Just walking past a cake shop can bring us unstuck.

(Remember those Donald Duck cartoons when a little devil duck and angel duck popped out of his head and argued about what he should do?) We are not just one person, born intact; rather, we are raised by other humans who we have taken into our being; we have special neurons called mirror neurons specifically to carry out this internalisation of role models. So, by adulthood, we are essentially a bundle of all the people, good and bad, who have influenced or impacted our lives. And this disparate crowd rarely get along.

The first thing is to figure out who is in there. If one or both of your parents, or another carer, was harsh and judgmental, then you will probably have that kind of voice in your head. 'Buck yourself up', 'You useless sod.' If you are feeling miserable at any given time, a useful thing to do is to check if this sub-personality has seized the microphone. Also, in most people's make-up there will likely be a spirited but rather brainless *defiant self* – what Billy Connolly once called a 'rebel without a clue'. This sub-personality will argue with traffic signs and start fights that can only end in tears. This part of your nature is useful to break out of a rut (and of course it has a vital job in adolescence to bust you out of your family), but it is not someone you really want in charge. The rebel in you knows what it does *not* want to be or do. It is not so good at making forward choices.

Finally, in most of us there is also a seductive, helpless, baby-voiced self, skilful at getting other people to rescue them, or a whingeing, self-pitying version of the same thing. Wound-licking has its place. Admitting you need help is an important aspect of maturity. But these are mind states for bringing change about and then moving on; they are not a recipe for mature self-reliance or true empowerment.

Not all the people in your head are negative, hopefully you have many helpful ones. A kind, encouraging self. A logical Mr Spock self. A fun, spontaneous, playful self. These three selves make quite a good team together – warm, wise and full of life.

Didi Bark, an English Steiner educator, now in her eighties, who first got me thinking about this, gave the parts of herself *playful names* so that she could manage the crowd inside her head.

(Didi was the height of respectability, and so it knocked me sideways that one of hers was 'Charlotte the Harlot.') I learned this trick from her and I use it often to disarm the more toxic occupants of my skull. Wild horses couldn't drag these out of me, but you might have fun designating your own version of Helpless Harry, Vindictive Vern, Grasper the Greedy Ghost, or Simon Smartarse and his brother Pompous Pete. Once spotted, they are easily sent back to their corner and you can have fun with the better denizens of your mind.

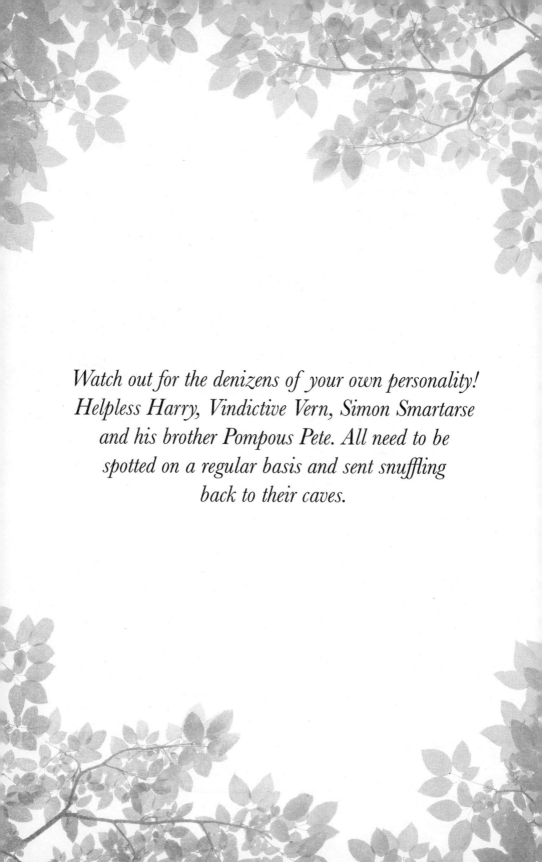

*Watch out for the denizens of your own personality!
Helpless Harry, Vindictive Vern, Simon Smartarse
and his brother Pompous Pete. All need to be
spotted on a regular basis and sent snuffling
back to their caves.*

7

SPECIAL SECTION

Delivering the Male

Note: This is one of our breakout sections, applying what we have learned to problems that most readers – and the world at large – are facing with some urgency. This special section tackles the terrible and seemingly intractable problem of 'messed-up men' and how to create maleness that is life-affirming, gentle and kind. Fully human men are something women and children long for and the whole world badly needs. For our Earth to survive, we have to get masculinity right. And, the thing is, *we do know how.* This has been much of my life's work. But let me start with a personal story, from long, long ago . . .

Our schooldays had ended. Suddenly, I was rarely seeing the friends I had spent every day with for the past six years. The looming prospect of university, in equal parts exciting and terrifying, was kept at bay by the familiar rituals of an Australian summer. Then, out of the blue, the phone call came. It was one of my friends, but he sounded odd; something had happened. He was so rattled that he got his message back to front. There was to be a funeral; one of our friends had died. It was a shooting accident. Our class teacher had asked several classmates to let the rest of us know. I put the phone down and just sat, stunned and numb.

The service, held the very next day, was ghastly. Girls from our class were weeping and distraught. I caught sight of what must have been David's parents: a mother looking haunted, a father mute and stiff. The minister did his best, but, not knowing the family, he could only speak in platitudes: 'We are reminded of another David . . .' In my dulled, Asperger's brain always struggling with social comprehension, something like anger stirred. This wasn't right. We shuffled out into the bright sunshine, wordless, and stumbled off home.

I hadn't even contemplated yet that my friend might have killed himself. He was an amiable boy, but also the smartest, easily topping the school's exam results. In the way of 1960s schoolboys, our group joked around all day without ever saying anything about our inner worlds; we recounted the TV shows we had seen the night before, had philosophical debates, managed the odd friendly word to an actual girl, or were the bemused subject of their jokes or flirtations. But I have a specific memory of David that has stayed with me through the decades that followed. It was a moment of unusual kindness.

I lived about four miles from school and cycled in each day. On this morning, there had been strong headwinds, and, in some kind of hormonal spin, I had set off very early and flogged along, pushing myself too hard. I arrived at the still almost-deserted school, so winded that I soon realized I was going to throw up. Heaving over a rubbish bin near my locker, I dimly noticed David about ten metres away. He walked up and put a hand on my shoulder, as I stood gasping for breath, looking at the remains of my breakfast among the crisp packets. Being comforted by a classmate in the 1960s, let alone being touched in any way other than thumps and bumps, was so unusual, and so much what I needed at that moment, that I can still feel that hand on my shoulder fifty years on.

My mother learned on the grapevine a few weeks after the event that his death had not been accidental, but acknowledging that was hard for me, because it was incomprehensible. He had been absolutely committed to academic success, to mastering the science-heavy curriculum; all of us lived for science, its safe world of rules and certainties. He had chosen to die on the day before university began. Clearly, this was a threshold he was not able to cross. Yet it had been the goal of his life. Nothing added up.

Only decades later did it occur to me that someone might know. As soon I could, I returned to Melbourne and found the office where the coroner's records were kept. A kindly woman retrieved a folder from the expander files stretching into the darkness. She looked at me and said gently, pausing slightly before handing it over, 'I noticed the cause of death, and just wanted to warn you, *there might be photographs.*'

There was nothing of the kind. The file was shocking only in its brevity. It described, as such reports must, the physical details of how he had ended his life. It ended with the standard euphemism, 'No suspicious circumstances.' Again, I felt the anger I had felt at the funeral, thirty years before. How could they leave it at that? What had happened to my friend? I'm no closer to knowing that today. A murder can take years of work by teams of people to 'solve.' But kill yourself and nobody bothers to investigate why.

Of course, we know that being a teenager is hard. There are cultures where this is not the case, but ours is so deficient at supporting the transition from child to adult that we've made adolescence into a no-man's-land that is so terrifying to cross. We just don't provide the sense of safety and connection from caring adults, especially adults beyond the family. Boys and girls alike cower in the trenches. Many are wounded, some fatally. Youth suicide, which had fallen for decades, recently began to steadily climb, and boys 'succeed' in this act at more than double the rate for girls.

My own teens, like yours no doubt, had aspects both unique and universal. One feature of a 1960s youth was the almost complete absence of touch. I had caring and stable parents, but the language between parents and kids in those days did not extend to hugs. As little kids, we had loved sitting on the lap of our dad, a working-class man, more at home being physical than verbal; he adored us kids, and he was funny and kind. But my mum was from that social tier of people who were stiff and awkward in their bodies. My strongest memories of touch were as a toddler, being held on a large, chilly toilet seat, my mother crouched before me, to prevent me falling in. I remember the closeness of these moments and prolonging the experience as best I could! My mum was well into her sixties when my sister and I eventually persuaded her to let us hug her, to soften her body instead of tightening it up and half-strangling us, and, once she softened, she loved it and never missed a hug thereafter.

By thirteen or fourteen, childhood over, you could go for months without a single person doing more than brush inadvertently against your clothing, let alone skin on skin. Anthropologists have noted the extreme lack of touch in some cultures and its correlation with violence. Yet, in indigenous, hunter-gatherer societies, being held, carried, cuddled as a child was as normal as breathing. In Asia, to this day, male friends hold hands in the street. In Indian homes I have visited, the kids were barely ever away from affectionate touch. Right into young adulthood, same-sex siblings and friends drape around each other in soothing connection. Travelling in Calcutta one dark night, I fell into a deep hole; my hosts pulled me out in concern and patted me all over with their hands, as if I were play dough and they were putting me back in one piece.

Touch brings a sense of being alive, an extraordinary soothing effect, endorphins and serotonin flow freely, calming both body and brain. (So-called 'comfort foods' replicate this effect on the inner 'skin' of one's digestive tract, which has the same wiring and origins as the outer skin of our bodies. Millions of people eat as a substitute for touch.)

My teacher, Virginia Satir, the originator of family therapy, famously said you need three hugs a day for survival, six to thrive and grow. 'Skin hunger' was the term used by the psychologist Harry Harlow, who famously studied infant monkeys, which, without affectionate mothering, became zombie-like and profoundly disturbed.

Satir taught that touch both affirms your existence and your intrinsic worth and creates a sense of vitality and energy. It is a primal signal of inclusion in the human race. It settles agitation and creates trust. Today, we know the health benefits of dogs in hospitals and schools, and in my backyard are two rescue dogs who rush me each morning for a welter of head scratching and fur ruffling. I don't think teenagers need touch any less than dogs do.

My Asperger's condition of course complicated this. To connect with people, especially girls, required some basic facility in verbal exchange. (Even that sentence sounds autistic as I read it back!) My attempts at conversation, made with good humour and warm intent (I was not a cold fish, even though I was well out of water), simply failed to land. I loved school, because it had structure and I knew how to do that, but unstructured time was a nightmare. I barely knew how to walk, or where to stand, or what face to wear.

In those days, church youth groups and camps were a feature of many teen lives. One frosty morning, at a camp somewhere in the Dandenong Ranges, I was up early, mooching about. A young couple I knew were standing by the fireplace in long coats. Always together, they had their arms around each other, and were quietly serene, waiting for breakfast. The girl, towered over by her boyfriend, but easily the most expressive of the two, saw me, smiled, and did a remarkable thing. She extended her arm, clearly inviting me to join them, drawing me into her side to be part of the hug.

We stood there for several minutes, two lanky young men and this sparky young woman between us, one on each shoulder, gazing at the fire, uttering the odd word from time to time. I could feel her warmth radiating into every cell of my body, soothing away my aloneness. I had felt increasingly at this age that, if I died, nobody, including me, would really mind. Touch made me want to stay alive.

It is a fair bet that my friend, whatever the reasons for ending his own life, could have been saved if a small group of friends had simply listened to his worries, hung out with him until he got through it, and above all been happy to cradle him in their arms and stroke or massage him back into wanting to live. Those friendly girls who we grew up around us would have helped, if they'd even known that was what was needed. He knew touch mattered, or he would not have come over to comfort me that morning.

MEN NEED REAL-WORLD HELP

For many years, we have taken the view that men take their lives because of their inability to open their hearts. So their friends just have no idea, and cannot help them. We assume that suicide is death from loneliness. While that is certainly true, in practical terms, it is not enough simply to encourage men to be vulnerable, because what if nobody responds?

Attempts have been made to make men feel less ashamed of not coping, through describing it as an actual illness – depression – and treating it with medication primarily, unless they are well off or lucky enough to also have psychological help or counselling. But depression can be a natural response to life being lonely and to the feelings of failure brought on by the narrow roles we impose on men.

In fact, very often men do seek help, but those around them are either so stunned or so unused to being supportive in a male-friendly way, they clam up again and feel even worse. The health and mental health services are still woefully inadequate, both in provision and in expertise in this field.

Current thinking is that, rather than simply having campaigns for men to open up, we have to provide very targeted services around the three crisis areas in men's lives that are evident in all the research:

1. Separation and marriage breakdown.
2. Drug and alcohol abuse.
3. Unemployment or financial stress.

Small, local, male-friendly help services that are practical *and* emotionally supportive, and have expertise in these specific areas, look like they are the best form of suicide prevention.

In Australia, a great programme called MENDS works with newly separated men to help them stabilize and learn from their marriage break-up experience, so that they can be more successful in relationships in future, and also build a calm, strong base to continue to be a good father to their children. Dads in Distress is a self-help network that also sustains and educates men at what is usually the worst crisis of their lives, and the one most risky for their wellbeing.

We are just beginning to care, intelligently and sensitively, for boys and men, and treat them as valuable and feeling beings with unique needs. If we want them to be empathic and open-hearted husbands, fathers, brothers and sons, then we have to treat them that way.

In this chapter, we will look at how the Four-Storey Mansion is essential in the rehabilitation of men. And how women's lives are so hugely affected by men's centuries of damage. I hope, if you are a woman reading this, that you gain a sense of clarity and empathy for what men are undergoing, what has made them the way they are and how they can be supported to heal. But that healing is our own responsibility, and at last we men are addressing it.

I would reckon on 90 per cent of women's woes having a male at the heart of them. And, more widely than that, the competitive, aggressive, individualistic nature of our society clearly reflects male pathology. Women who succeed in it often do so by becoming male-like in their values and methods. The worldwide response to New Zealand PM Jacinda Ardern shows that there is a non-patriarchal way of doing politics, economics and much more. On the first day of her leadership, another woman MP advised her to go on the attack. Ms Ardern replied clearly and definitively, 'I'm sorry, but that's just not me.'

Women have a huge stake in male rehabilitation. In Australia, where I live, a country of twenty-five million people, a woman is killed by a man on average once a week. But self-violence is vastly more common. Six men a day take their own lives, and 32,000 ambulance call-outs annually are for men who have made attempts. In the UK things are somewhat better, suicide rates are gradually falling, and the country is about in the middle of world rankings. But it still claims twelve men's lives each day. At almost treble the road-accident toll, it's still a shocking loss of life.

Several years ago in the town where I then lived, some friends of a man, a newly retrenched public servant, were called by his distraught wife to his house. He had a gun, was ranting and weeping uncontrollably. The friends slept in shifts at his house for several days (while his wife and children went elsewhere), talking, soothing, quietly disputing his arguments. Someone was always awake and with him; the gun had long been taken away. The crisis passed, and he was profoundly grateful to them. Today, he helps men in similar situations, as a volunteer, and he can barely believe how close he came to disaster.

Right now, a new masculinity is clearly emerging – men have trebled the time they spend with their children in the last thirty years, many men freely cry or hug their friends, and a younger generation relates with an easy equality to their partners, or women in general. Being gay or transgender doesn't faze or threaten them one bit. That's the cutting edge. But a large and ugly rump is still to be shifted, across many cultures. It's a planet-wide task, and we have to address it now.

WHAT WENT WRONG?

It's worth getting to the roots of how maleness went so adrift and took our whole society with it. Let's see if we can do this in just a page. For 300,000 years, an almost unimaginable reach of time, humans lived in a very specific and unchanging way. We lived in small close-knit clans, where everyone was related, and cared about and protected each other. Life was precious – for most of prehistory, humans were very small in number: in the whole British Isles, in the first interglacial period, there were only around 5,000 people.

A boy growing up in that long-ago past had a whole team of men – uncles, grandfathers, as well as a dad – who taught and guided him, almost full-time, every day. They had to, because by age fourteen he would be a man, and everyone's lives depended on him being safe, skilful and selfless. The proper initiation of boys into being good men was a prominent part of every culture on Earth.

Masculinity was passed on like a river from one generation

to the next. These were matriarchal societies, and the teaching of boys focused on the nurture and protection of life around them. I was privileged to spend time as a young man in West New Britain with people like this, and witnessed the gentleness and cohesion of a society barely touched by the Age of Empires. When humans moved into an agricultural way of life, life got a lot tougher and more austere, and the role of women was debased – the beginnings of patriarchy arrived. Yet, on the whole, people still lived in community, and boys had tuition in manhood that was detailed and had sacred dimensions.

Then, within our own living memory almost, this changed too. We moved to an industrial way of life, and suddenly men and children were separated for almost the whole of the day. Men went down coal mines, into factories and mills. They were taken away to fight in catastrophic wars that killed millions, and those who came back were damaged and mute. Many older men today remember this as the backdrop of their lives. A remote father, either alcoholic or violent, or both, obsessed with control, lashing out. Or the other extreme – inadequate and crushed.

But the need for fathering is wired into every child – boy or girl. Every child craves a dream father who loves, teaches, encourages and affirms him. But when the world industrialized, the time for this was lost. Many fathers became like an ogre, a frightening man who showed up at your house at night. And a rift, huge and nameless, spread through the homes and families of the nineteenth and twentieth centuries. Robert Bly called it the father-wound.

Boys no longer were fathered, or uncled, to even one-tenth

of what their minds and hearts needed for wholeness. Women did their best, and that was often very good, but that small but essential keystone of a boy's masculinity was missing. A generation of men grew up who did not know the inner world of older men, how to navigate in a male body, with its unique chemistry, needs and joys.

Women on their own can raise boys to be wonderful men, and they have done this for thousands of years. But the ones who fare best usually seek out good men to be in their sons' lives – grandads, uncles, the guitar teacher, the sports coach, the gay man next door. They are judicious, of course, and it helps if we men are available and know this is our job – that 'fathering' is a shared activity. A boy needs to experience every kind of masculinity they can, so that from these examples he can bundle together the unique kind of man that it is in his soul to be. It's hard to be a good man, if you have never really seen one.

By the end of the twentieth century, nine out of ten men were not close to their fathers, many actively hated them. The father-wound ran like a Grand Canyon through our culture, and we just thought that was how it had to be.

Fixing It with Your Father

In the chapter on emotions we talked about men who were moved to reconcile with their estranged dads, this was a brave and risky thing to do. The safest way by far to do this was by simply asking, 'What was it like for you, when we were kids?'

'What was going on, back then?' Not accusing, just wanting to understand. It was often a revelation. One man, a surgeon, travelled from Australia back to the UK and found his father (whom he had hated in childhood and not seen for thirty years) dying in a nursing home. He rented a flat and stayed with him there, so that he could die in peace. His letter telling me about this, and thanking me, is one of the most precious things I own.

Men need other men to learn from and lean on, and to help them grow a wider, more comfortable masculinity. And to not burden the women in our lives with carrying the emotions for us. Men most urgently need to live on all four floors of our mansion. At sixty-seven, speaking personally, I still need the nourishment of men older than me, regularly, in my life; it makes me calm and it makes me braver. I don't expect to ever outgrow that need.

What Does a Good Man Look Like?

What makes a good man? I once asked an audience of 200 women, who were able to call out (with some ribald asides) all of the following and many more . . .

- gentleness
- kindness
- consideration

- safe
- honest
- reliable
- trustworthy
- fun
- generosity of spirit and heart
- practical
- hard-working
- open-hearted
- loving
- positive
- patient
- even-tempered

It was somewhat poignant to hear the intensity with which some of the women spoke. You could tell they had experienced the opposite, in many cases, and it had sharpened their yearning for something else. And no doubt men would have a similar list.

Once the list had been generated, I pointed out something important. Every quality falls into one of two categories: backbone and heart. A good man has to have both. Loving, clearly, is heart, but reliability is backbone. One without the other is no use. You can have a kind, funny and gentle man who is hopelessly unreliable, not true to this word and can't be counted on. Many readers will have had one of these for a father or former husband. Or you can have a reliable, solid and organized man, who is wooden and cold, too stingy and

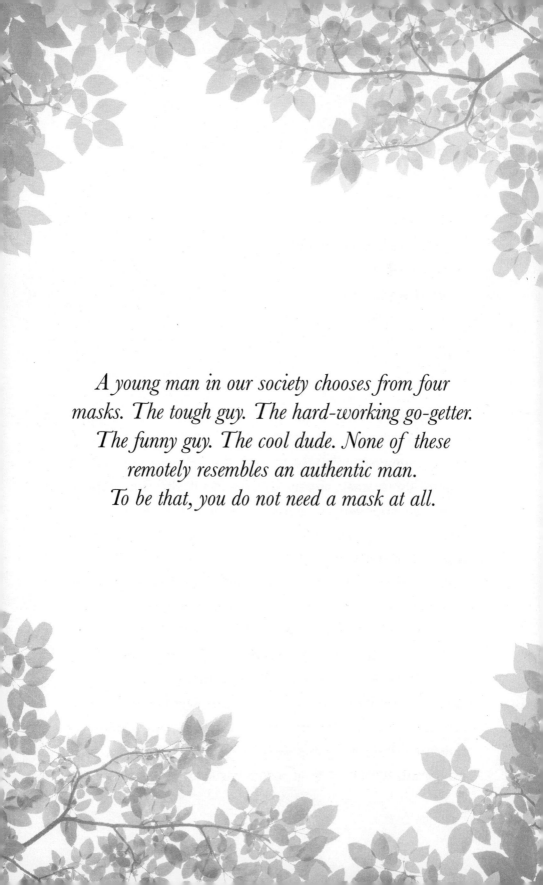

A young man in our society chooses from four masks. The tough guy. The hard-working go-getter. The funny guy. The cool dude. None of these remotely resembles an authentic man. To be that, you do not need a mask at all.

rule-bound to be nourishing for you or his children. He will be there, but you just aren't sure you want him to be. In terms of our Four-Storey Mansion, he never leaves the third floor. He lives in his head, cut off from his heart and balls.

In raising our sons, we have to ensure they have both backbone and heart. A man with real strength of character, who can stick with it through hard times, but also knows when to laugh and read you poetry, is not too much to ask for.

Dropping the Mask

'Fixing it with your father' is one important step. The other is learning to 'drop the mask'. To be able to emerge from the shell put on in adolescence and be real.

Imagine a boy of fourteen today. Puberty is well underway; the outer changes are obvious, but on the inside, the effects are also great. His levels of testosterone, which began to stir at twelve, at first making him dreamy and disorganized, are now at full steam, around 800 per cent higher than in his primary-school years. He is jumping out of his skin. But what are we doing to harness that energy and bless it, or make it sacred?

He feels the expectation to grow up and 'be a man' coming at him like a train. But he does not really have the 'software', the inside story, of how to be male. Unless he is very lucky, his dad and other men in his circle work long hours and only spend small amounts of time with their children. And when they do, they are not very talkative, certainly not about inner feelings, dreams or stories. Perhaps a few teachers at school are a bit more giving of themselves. A boy at this age wants to appear manly and able to stand tall in his social world, but he doesn't really know how. What is he to do?

Unless some uncles or friends of his dad, or a caring teacher or two step up, he may be at a loss. There is only one way to create his identity: to fake it. There are a handful of standard male 'masks', or roles, he can get 'off the shelf'. If he grows up in a poor part of town where the young men are violent or aggressive, then he too must put on *the tough-guy* mask.

If his circumstances are slightly better, and he is more socially confident, perhaps he can manage the second standard mask – *the cool dude.* Sunglasses on head. Snappy clothes. Nice car. Matching girlfriend. Again, this role can be dropped, down the track, without any serious harm. Egotism, while ridiculous, is rarely fatal.

If he is not great-looking, or has some other deficit to cover up, but has a quick mind, he can be *the funny guy*, the jokester who breaks the tension, mocks himself and is always upbeat. Freer in some ways to be unconventional, but prone to depression behind the mask. This is the most suicide-prone of the mask choices.

Mask option number four is *the hard-working go-getter*, who is not so sociable, but can get ahead of the rest. Some girls quite like these boys; they're not so exciting, but a good team-mate in chasing material success – if that's what you want. By now, we are into the corporate world, and the majority of white-collar men. There is less chance of dying, unless you include dying of boredom!

Gay men tell me they too have standard masks to adopt, which are different but equally limiting, and so important to drop as one becomes more secure.

The problem with masks is clear – the real person is not seen. But, if we are not seen, we do not connect. We shrivel up. What works in the big world does not work in the intimate sphere. Partners hungry for real intimacy start to despair of it ever happening, children don't feel loved or connected. A masked man at the dinner table does not nourish or reassure. Teenage boys find themselves being inexplicably angry with their fathers, not knowing it's because they just want more from him.

Thankfully, all this is starting to change. A while back, a video clip went viral on the Internet, of French tennis star Nicolas Mahut sitting with tears in his eyes, moments after losing a vital match. Suddenly, his young son runs from the stands and hugs his dad. The fans erupt in affirmation, and his opponent Leonardo Mayer himself is teary and empathic looking on. When I came across this footage, it had already had seven million views. Being real is something that people today literally applaud. It's so unusual.

How to remove the mask? It's as simple as admitting when you are stumped. Afraid. Embarrassed. Sad. Mistaken. Not being afraid to go to your second floor and feel. This is often termed 'vulnerability', but the ability to be open is also a kind of strength. Sorrow, grief, embarrassment and even shame (the most difficult emotion for men to feel) are all a process, and when we've passed through them many times, we discover that they are nourishing and necessary to growth. And all that women ask of men is that they be willing to grow.

There's an odd strength in being able to say, with real openness, 'I am not in a good place, but I am able to be at one with that, I am not ashamed of it. I will find my way. And your help and support are welcome.' And then the work of building yourself a real masculinity, true to yourself, can begin.

It was thirty years ago, now, that I wrote *Manhood*. That first edition showed an eagle on the cover, flying across a skyscraper with hundreds of identical windows. A man wrote to me that behind every window was a man dreaming of escape. If you are a man reading this, I hope you will walk out of the glass prison that traps you. Get down into your body and dance and move, shudder and ache. Move up to your heart and inhabit all the rooms of emotion. And get out of your tiny skull into the wild winds and freedom of spirit.

If you are a woman, there's a fair chance you have hoped and prayed for masculine change, in your own relationships and in the world. The thought that the men in your world – fathers, husbands, sons and workmates – could be different, happier, safer, more trusting, kinder, is such a heartfelt wish. Really, the world depends on it happening fast. I hope this book on being Fully Human helps that along.

8

THE FOURTH FLOOR

Spirituality Is Not What You Think

It's been rainy for days, but on Sunday morning the sun pokes through. He walks into the kitchen and says to her, 'It's looking fine outside, how about we go to the beach?' She hesitates, frowns, looks at their two small children squabbling in the living room, and then on impulse says, 'Oh, why not?' They drive to a quiet bay that they know, and walk along the beach, their dog running ahead. At the end of the bay, they stop and rest. The children play in the rock pools, utterly absorbed. Suddenly tired, he lies down, hat over his face. She goes for a walk a bit further on. Later, walking back along the water's edge, she takes his hand. She hasn't done that for a while. As they drive home, the kids fall asleep in their seats.

So much that we do is not logical,
on the surface. Walking on beaches, growing
flowers, lavishing affection on a dog. But it's
actually the very heart of what makes life work.

A visitor from another planet would watch much human activity and be baffled as to its purpose. So much that we do is not logical, on the surface. Walking on beaches, growing flowers, lavishing affection on a dog. But it's actually the very heart of what makes life work.

Here is a puzzling question: what do those, and the following activities, all have in common? Surfing, skateboarding or riding mountain bikes. Getting drunk. Working really hard on a hobby or project. Going to music festivals and rock concerts. Going to church. Making love. Using drugs. Joining a meditation class or retreat. Hiking up a mountain. Swimming naked in the moonlight. Going to a football match. Putting on headphones and dancing about in your living room. Playing an exciting computer game. Making music. Making art. Having one brief, intense night of love. Committing to a long-term relationship. Having and raising a family.

What they have in common will shock you. All of the above are, at their very heart, spiritual pursuits. (And I left out some more challenging ones.) Of course, if you asked the person doing any of the above, 'Why do you do it?' they would rarely be shocked. They would say, 'Because I love doing it, it makes me feel good.' But the *reason* it makes them feel good, if explored, would lead to something like, 'I feel most alive, most whole, most out of my usual self, when I do that activity.'

Spiritual pursuits are actions taken in order to lose our sense of separateness and to be part of the whole. The whole of the ocean, the whole of the football crowd, the whole auditorium pulsing to the beat, the whole of the wheeling sky above. (Of course, some of the things humans do to feel good can be terribly dysfunctional, or do terrible harm. But even the most evil actions – violence, abuse, destruction – still originate in trying to reach that feeling of release and peace.) These apparently non-rational actions that most humans simply can't get enough of, and will cross oceans to experience, have a single goal: to make us feel at home in the universe, and hopefully carry some of that feeling back to normal life.

In the Beginning

When we are a baby, or a small child, if things are going even half well, we feel for much of the time absolutely secure, and delighted – connected to our mother's arms and body, to her smiles and cuddles. This soon broadens out to the things around the home and the backyard, our dad's deep voice and playfulness, perhaps brothers and sisters. In Laurie Lee's extraordinary memoir *Cider with Rosie*, this feeling is described by a little boy growing up in the pre-industrial world of the valleys behind Stroud, in Gloucestershire. Tall hollyhocks crowding above him, his big sisters' rowdy care, the noise and tumult of a big, poor family.

We start off part of it all. Then somehow, through the impositions and deprivations of modern life, it begins to get more distant. We are not always held, not always nurtured, words begin to replace reality, and we grow away from the direct

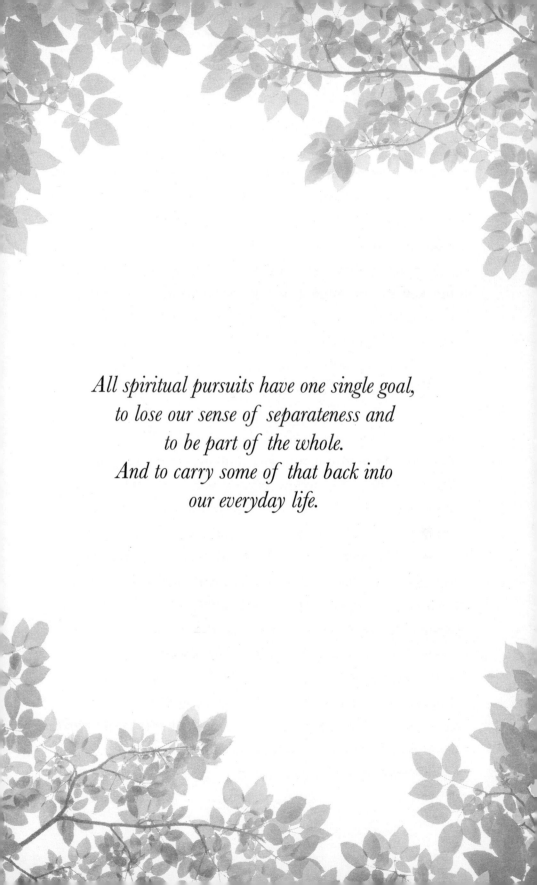

*All spiritual pursuits have one single goal,
to lose our sense of separateness and
to be part of the whole.
And to carry some of that back into
our everyday life.*

experience of nature and love. Human beings are always, at heart, motivated by the wish to return to, or discover union with the world around them. (Almost everything on our list, at one time or another – from wild sexuality to surfing or using hallucinogenics – was acknowledged and accredited as a religious practice.)

Spirituality – feeling merged and at home, not separate – is the key to our mental and physical health. The problem, though, with many secular-but-still-spiritual activities is that we may not fully take the benefits on, because we are ignorant of what is available. A person might make love with their partner with no more meaning or depth than eating a hamburger. Being spiritually ignorant, they do it to get it done, and shut down their body and heart to the depth of what is available. In fact, they may be frightened by the intensity they sense around sexuality, and may actively work to dispel unsettling feelings of tenderness to their partner, or vulnerability in themselves. (In *Manhood* we explored the rather shocking insight that most men – in lovemaking with their partners – ejaculate, and think that is pretty good, but never truly have an orgasm. They are just too tense in their bodies, too self-conscious, and so all sensation is locked in a small part of their body. They never surrender or open themselves enough to experience even 10 per cent of what it is possible to feel. The orgasms depicted in pornography and even in mainstream movies are portrayed by men who have this limited experience; they resemble more a bad case of constipation!)

The problem with any of the things we do to 'feel better' is that, if we don't know their real purpose, then we don't take from it the proper benefits and perspective. We are not refreshed enough, opened enough, surrendered enough, and we don't learn enough from doing it for the effects to last. Making love with a sense of the sacred is a million miles from this; it's as if both people invoke ancient forces of creation and find in each other a merging with the stars, their animal selves are released, there is a celebration of intimacy and trust, and lots of laughter.

Anything Can Be Sacred

Anything we do can be – to use religious language – 'dedicated to God', made sacred, made into an opening rather than a closing of our life force. Let's take the example of surfing (or mountain biking, skiing, or going to rave parties). Even the most unawakened young person can 'get' surfing as a blissful activity, and will drive for hours and wait in the shivering cold to experience it again, for what are really just a few seconds on the face of the wave. (But it could be croquet.) That fleeting second when it's all just flow.

The tragedy is that we don't quite know how to appreciate it on all its levels. And so young surfers can miss the meaning. An older acquaintance of mine made a surf movie, which he only completed after the tragic death of his son. He had included in the original version a quote: 'Life is a waste of time and surfing is a great way to waste it.' I had to confront him about this. Life is not a waste of time, and the last thing young people need is to be falsely initiated into nihilism. To speak in his defence, deep down he knew this; after grieving for his son, he devoted his life to nurturing young kids in the surf lifesaving world. He knew better than to spout such nonsense. We are here in this world for each other, and nothing could be further from being a waste of time.

So What About Religion?

The philosopher Alain de Botton believes that a lot of spiritual practice, ritual, mythology and the like has evolved simply because we are terrible at remembering – at holding on to the experience of heightened states of being. We slip out of the whole and get caught up in the small. So we worship, or celebrate, or participate in private or communal activity to bring it back. Religion, for all its terrible risks and failings, is an attempt to codify and organize an ongoing connection with the sacred. So our cathedrals are designed to resemble mighty forest glades, sunlight shafting in, impossibly high trunks and branches above us, unworldly beings painted on the walls and ceilings. Religion attempts what is probably impossible – to fix what is quicksilver and ineffable and make it repeatable and constant – but even trying to do so somehow manages, down the centuries, to be a help.

A few years ago, I was involved in the boldest, most likely-to-fail project I had ever taken on in my life – heading up a group of 300 schools and community groups in a four-year project to build an artwork almost half a kilometre long on the Canberra lakeshore. Not just any artwork, but a memorial to 300 refugee mothers and children, who lost their lives in a politically explosive tragedy off Australia's shores. (You can find out about it at www.sievxmemorial.com) During those four years, I was often terrified and out of my depth, but I found that listening to our rather exceptional minister at my local Uniting Church would restore and deepen my courage and conviction that what I was doing was right. Like most of my generation, I had found Christianity unbearable in its old forms, and spent decades away, but I was drawn back in through the examples of activism and engagement that seemed braver and more self-effacing than anything I had found elsewhere. Now, I was pushing against the tide of politics and significant hatred and bigotry in my country, but his preaching linked me into a tradition where that was exactly the right thing to do. Where my own comfort did not matter, and my smallness need not worry me at all. Striving for justice for refugees was a spiritual action, and courage and peace came from remembering that.

Organized religion is fraught, it has been hijacked and exploited and used as a cover for con artists for as long as it existed. (Jesus' main message when he arrived in Jerusalem at last was exactly that – denouncing the vested religious interests who had sold out his own country to the genocidal cruelties of empire.) And it's happening just as much today

– the American corporate right found fundamentalist religion
to be such a ripe harvest, a ready-made cache of gullibility
that they could round up for political fodder. But it happens
in every faith. In spite of that, good people won't surrender
their faith traditions, and they remain a body of understanding
and practice that can carry you when your personal limitations
mean you would never make it. It puts community around the
spiritual journey and says, 'People have walked these laby-
rinths before. You aren't alone.'

INTERFAITH – THE NEW SPIRITUALITY

There are two main ways in which people do spiritual practice.
Among most of my friends, the choice is to go it alone, pick
up a few bits here and there: a Buddhist retreat on Arran or
near Byron Bay; some serious yoga; some Celtic Christianity.
I admire and envy this, and it's been my way too, at times in
my life. It's a natural, healthy pantheism that keeps you free
of the traps of dogma and the odium of what religion has
come to represent to many in the West today – war, bigotry
and paedophilia. Organized religion has such a bad name for
many that it ranks alongside organized crime as a thoroughly
unpleasant thing we'd be better off without.

So we opt to make our own way, and that certainly has
integrity, and the richness of combining many traditions. The
shadow side of DIY spirituality, though, is that our ego is not
challenged, as we do the choosing and can stay in our comfort

zones more than might be good for us. It can drift into a kind of spiritual pick-and-mix, lacking commitment, depth or cohesion.

But a new development is happening around the world. Sometimes, it's been because of the coalition of forces coming together around the climate catastrophe we are facing. People are noticing that the best activism, and the bravest, often comes from religious people, who of course have a long tradition of standing up to power, and also of not being afraid of self-sacrifice. To many Christians, for example, toxic hypercapitalism is very familiar – it's the Roman Empire all over again.

People of faith recognize a common bond, whether we are Sikhs or Quakers. While simple-minded adherents to religion see it as all being about us and them, the one true faith, anyone with half a brain sees that the founders, the directly connected mystics who founded religions, were deeply inclusive and regarded each person and their path as being of equal worth. None of them had religion on their minds, those were just the fallible attempts to maintain the message. In spirituality, every path goes up the same mountain, or it would not be the true mountain, after all. If there is a binary in your faith, it's not of God. God does not do 'us and them'.

My hope is that people in future identify as interfaith, as a deliberate act of rebellion from both the emptiness of secularism and the bigotry of sectarianism. But they still *identify with their own tradition* as a matter of culture and identity. Indigenous people know the danger of obliteration – that if you pour your uniqueness into the river, all you get is river. We have to hold our own lineage dear.

I am a Christian because it's my heritage, an accident of birth, and not because I think it's better than any other faith tradition. Its missteps and atrocities horrify me, but I won't abandon it, and especially not to the hucksters and carpet-baggers of the right. The New Testament message was a leap forward in human history, the first religion to truly put compassion at its centre and value every living person, and it's little wonder that it was, for its first few centuries, a religion of women and slaves. Christians forever fall back into the pit of judging and excluding others – it's been the curse both of Catholicism and a thousand divided sects on the Protestant side. (A lovely joke is often told in Scotland, of a man who was shipwrecked, and when his rescuers came, they found he had built two churches. One to attend, and one to avoid on principle!) But thoughtful Christian writers, like Richard Rohr and the theologians behind the luminous *Living the Questions* DVD series, are crystal clear. There are no binaries in the kingdom of heaven. Nobody is cast out. If you find yourself feeling intolerant of anyone, look within.

A well-lived life is a communal life, and faith is a community that I suspect we all need if we are to be truly free.

But if bushwalking works for you just as well, go for it. The word 'recreation' is one we use glibly, so stop for a moment and think what that really means. Recreating yourself allows for both restoration and also a new beginning each time you do it, a new you.

The key is to make it sacred. To simply allow what you are doing to have that intention, that awareness. When done in a consciously open and receptive way, every one of the activities in our list will do the trick. Regular spiritual practice is practical – as real as money in the bank. You are building up a store-house, a reserve that you can then deploy against fears, suffering, moral challenges, weakness or disability – all the things that plague and diminish our lives – and face them with a sparkle in your eye. All you have to do is say, 'Along with food and shelter, exercise, laughter and love, the spiritual side of me needs to be fed and watered too.' People who do this find their life is transformed – at first gently, but then abso-lutely. And that makes all the difference.

The Place Where You Open

There are a handful of books that I have kept through many moves and travels, and would never want to part with. A surprising number of these are books about journeys in nature: Annie Dillard's *Pilgrim at Tinker Creek*; Jiang Rong's *Wolf Totem*, about life as an exile among the herders of Mongolia; Nan Shepherd's *The Living Mountain*; Brian Carter's aston-ishing novel *A Black Fox Running*; almost everything by Robert MacFarlane. But the most memorable of all is Peter Matthiessen's *The Snow Leopard*. This book comes closest to a perfect travelogue because it understands that every journey we make is on the inside as well as the outside. The word that reviewers return to again and again is 'luminous'.

The author of *The Snow Leopard* was not always a spiritual – or even, I suspect, an especially likeable – person. One gets the impression that his younger self was both arrogant and rather grouchy, perhaps even tormented. But he had a kind of honesty that was to stand him in good stead. And because it's very hard to write well about spirituality, I am going to tell his story here over a couple of pages, so you can learn through his journey.

Matthiessen was just getting to know the woman who would one day be his wife (the writer Deborah Love), when he returned home to New York from travelling away, to find three Zen monks waiting on her front doorstep. He was (according to his account in *Nine-Headed Dragon River*) mostly annoyed – who were these characters? At the time, he and Deborah were having problems and had not spoken for several months. The surprising collision of unexpected guests was all awkward-ness and fumbling, at least on the part of the couple, and he learned later that the two older monks, after he had gone, had 'shaken their shining heads and sighed "Poor Deborah!"'

But Matthiessen was an observant man, and the impression of the monks struck him so deeply that he could not get them out of his thoughts. By the time he wrote *The Snow Leopard*, he had not only become a Buddhist, but also one of the world's best chroniclers of the collision of Buddhism and the West. And he brought millions of readers along with him.

So what did he see in these diminutive men, even in that short encounter? Here are his words:

'Hakuun Yasutani-roshi, eighty-four years old, was a light, gaunt figure with hollowed eyes and round prominent ears; as I was to learn he had spent much of that morning upside down, standing on his head. Beside him, Nakagawa Soen-roshi . . . elfin and merry, entirely at ease and entirely aware at the same time, like a paused swallow, gave off emanations of lightly contained energy that made him seem much larger than he was.'

Even the younger monk-minder Tai-san, with his 'thick featured face and samurai bearing', nonetheless 'conveyed the same impression of contained power'.

Matthiessen had noted something that does indeed stand out in certain individuals. It's called 'presence'. These men, far from home in a Long Island street, somehow were intensely 'there'. I'd suspect this was their normal bearing when getting on a bus or going to the toilet. Their mind was in their body, and their body was in the present moment, and they had the calmness that such a long habit brings. For them, the term 'out of their comfort zone' did not exist. Within weeks, Matthiessen had enrolled to learn Zen meditation. He hated it, which can often be a promising sign. Eventually, he gave in to wild impulse and hiked across the Carmel mountains to the Buddhist Tassajara monastery, to train as a monk.

This is our first lesson on spirituality: *it shows*. It changes a person so fundamentally that almost anybody can tell. We know, on an animal level, when someone has their life together. We want to be like that too. We want some of that peace.

Getting There

Almost every religious tradition, before it became a band-wagon, an institution, was based on individuals seeking direct mystical experience. Perhaps we ought to get back to that idea. Jesus, Buddha, Mohammed, the shamans and mystics that abounded in the human story, rooted themselves in contacting the divine and letting that govern their actions in the world. Any of us can do spiritual practices, remembering that even a walk on the beach is as profound as any, if we understand its real purpose.

Matthiessen is self-deprecating and humble about the whole thing. On Zen, he writes, 'there is little that may sensibly be said about it without succumbing to that breathless mystery-ridden prose that drives so many sincere aspirants in the other direction'. But then, in the same sentence, he is crystal clear . . . Zen, he explains, is 'the moment by moment awakening of the mind'. Nothing more complex than that. Waking up.

In the foreword to *Nine-Headed Dragon River*, he does it again, in words that have stayed with me all my life . . .

'Zen has been called the "religion before religion," . . . the phrase evokes that natural religion of our early childhood, when heaven and a splendorous earth were one. But soon the child's clear eye is clouded over by ideas and opinions, preconceptions and abstractions. Simple free *being* becomes encrusted with the burdensome armor of the ego. Not until years later does an instinct come that a vital sense of mystery has been withdrawn. The sun glints through the pines, and the heart is pierced in a moment of beauty and strange pain, like a memory of paradise.'

The heart is pierced. (Once again, our body is talking to us. It's an actual pang, in the very centre of our life force.) Have you ever felt that? Sometimes in adolescence I felt that pain and thought it to be just the edge of a terrifying loneliness. In a way, it was, but it was also a threshold. If you feel something missing in your life, then there *must be something to be missed*. That moment of pain is the doorway to a belonging on the Earth that, with or without human company, is like a bustling, friendly house, where birds and animals, plants and sky are your long-lost family, welcoming you home.

One of my own now-grown children, often impacted by a lifelong pain condition, which in a lesser person might have led to despair, addiction or worse, has responded since early childhood to the presence of birds in a bush outside the window, or an eagle soaring above our mountain farm. They feel a warmth of actual kinship, as if the birds were cheery friends. Many other people are like that with animals, and it's not a big step from there to being at home with all of life.

The pangs of unexplained longing can be frightening, so we may flee into random activity to ward them off. But what they are is a crack in our composure, our ego armour; they are something that we can and should 'follow'. I can't emphasize enough how important it is to notice the feelings evoked by a glimpse of beach, or the outline of a tree through the mist, or distant clouds moving fast in a nighttime sky. Or a sudden urge to create music or art, or writing. Those feelings are your own soul saying, 'Follow me, discover yourself.'

Matthiessen continues,

'After that day, at the bottom of each breath, there is a hollow place that is filled with longing. We become seekers without knowing that we seek, and at first, we long for something "greater" than ourselves, something apart and far away. It is not a return to childhood, for childhood is not a truly enlightened state. Yet to seek one's own true nature is, as one Zen master has said, "a way to lead you to your long-lost home".'

Notice he says, 'at first'. Gradually, we realize that what we seek is much closer. It was right beside us all the time.

So here is our second lesson on spirituality. You already have inside you the keys – you feel a wordless, inexplicable sense of longing – a real physical ache, which you might rush to fill up with sex, or addiction, or any number of compulsive life choices, such as hard work, success, pleasures of every kind. And you end up back where you started, empty again. Instead, sit with that longing. Beyond the pain, the loneliness, the feeling of lack of purpose or meaning, is the truth which is its mirror image. There is love, there is meaning, there is purpose, there is peace. *You hunger for it because you know it is there.*

For many of us, romantic love is the form that the divine seems to take. This is very tricky ground, as a young person especially can mistake the gifts of love – that joy of adoring and being adored, the sense of melting into another person, and of course the sexual ecstasy of lovemaking – with the idea that this man or this woman is the possessor of our happiness. We should first admire a young person, in a world that preaches impersonality and using others as objects, that they are so open-hearted and willing to let go of their hard boundaries. But as adults, we should be clear that love is a portal through which a couple can pass, or a fire we can light together – we help each other experience the divine, but we are not each other's gods or goddesses. That distinction is what makes a marriage or relationship strong and growing, since we work with our human failings compassionately and resolutely. There is only one direction for a statue on a pedestal to fall. The secret is not to put anyone up there in the first place, or to let anyone else do that to you.

Robert Bly points this out in his aptly titled *A Little Book of the Human Shadow*. We men glimpse someone across a crowded room and are captivated. It's more than just desire, it's a feeling that she is some kind of goddess – the way she speaks, tosses her head, she is bewitching – but there is something transcendent there as well. 'Never follow up on this,' he cautions. 'She is your own inner divine feminine, and no real woman should be burdened with the weight of this expectation.' Putting this projection onto a real, human, fallible woman will only hurt her, and hurt you. Go to the beach for a week alone, he advises. Walk in the mountains. Take a notebook and start to write. Dive into yourself. A part of you is needing attention, it's been neglected, and might even be dying. But its perfume is suddenly there, and you must follow it down. This is not about yearning for a human soulmate. There is no such thing. You can be wonderful friends, but only you can be your own soul's mate. It's about finding your lost self.

So, dear reader, we will return to this many times. But, just for a moment, let your heart soften and ache with that yearning of all yearnings. For your long-lost home. Consider how that might be worth some time, and some effortless attention, lest it slip away. For this is a place that, once found, can be lived in more and more, and you can start to feel at ease in the world and in life. In your own skin. It's not easy, but it's remarkably simple. And the way to reach this place is simply to stop rushing about, and wait for it to arrive. To be here, now.

How It's Done

Neither Peter Matthiessen nor I would want to convert you to Zen or any other specific methodology. There is a way to suit everyone. Christianity's desert fathers and mothers, and its medieval mystics like Teresa of Ávila or Julian of Norwich, knew this road, so did the Sufis in Islam, Jewish mystics, and shamans in every place and time across the long prehistory of the world. Every indigenous clan or tribe had its young warriors, rash and bombastic, reined in and steered by a wise man or wise woman, a Gandalf to their Boromir. You can even be an atheist mystic, if that's what suits you best.

The actual method, as well as the goal, of every spiritual path, even if we shy from that very word, is always the same. To be present. Matthiessen writes, 'To practice Zen means to realize one's existence moment after moment, rather than letting life unravel in regret of the past and daydreaming of the future'. So here is our third message: beware of religious affectation of any brand, because at bottom they all share the same destination – a losing of one's separateness into the very heart of life.

Religion, Matthiessen writes, 'is only another idea to be discarded, like "enlightenment", and like "the Buddha" and like "God".'

Losing one's separateness solves every human agony. What is suicide but the most desperate loneliness? What is violence but the most terrible urge to find peace? We suffer because we feel estranged from life. Yet release from this is always there. Rattled by what I see on the TV or in my Facebook feed, I wander out to my garden and weed the radishes. I can feel peacefulness flowing from the soil. My brain starts to shape a response.

The Fear of Letting Go

Don't think this merging or surrender means taking anything away from who you are. We are here as us, and our individuality, our discernment, our unique way of thinking, our talents and our contribution, our pain and the lessons we have learned at such great cost are all to be celebrated. We are here to dance our own dance. But at the same time, we are like leaves of grass, bowing in the wind, and the beauty and rightness comes from doing that in harmony with all the other unique, special, living and non-living beings in the wheeling universe. Here is our fourth message then, and the final one. You are separate, and you are not. Both are true, but just on different levels of your Four-Storey Mansion. Every river, every tributary, every tiny creek is so distinctive that the salmon can smell it through a thousand miles of ocean. But a river surely feels joy to be back in the sea.

Being present in this way does not mean being 'still' in the sense of empty headed and passive. The still centre is a dynamic place, it's where creativity, good ideas, courage, health and inventiveness come from, but they come with an integrity and fittingness that makes them work. Sometimes almost without effort. From being present comes love for all our fellow creatures, and action to care for them.

John O'Donohue, a Catholic priest and poet, says that there is no such thing as the spiritual 'journey', and he speaks somewhat scathingly of spiritual programmes or curricula. The journey to enlightenment, he smiles, is a quarter of an inch long. In fact, it's as thin as rice paper. You just have to let it in. The answer's clear: your peace has always been right here.

Zen is a bootcamp route up the spiritual mountain, which might appeal to some. But, for me, the way taught by Vietnamese monk Thich Nhat Hanh is more compatible with the daily life that most of us lead – parenthood, work, housekeeping, marriage, action in the world.

Hanh was a young, engaged and activist Buddhist monk in South Vietnam during the worst years of the Vietnam War. He recruited thousands of young people to repair the damage of that war to villages and towns, building and staffing medical clinics, and quietly opposing the violence on both sides. Often his compatriots were killed, and he eventually had to flee the country. He came to the West in 1976. It was Hanh who persuaded Martin Luther King to speak out against the Vietnam War, a huge tactical risk for his civil rights work, and he was nominated by King for a Nobel Prize. Writer Thomas Merton and he were close friends. A shy-seeming man, with a voice almost like a whisper, Hanh was somehow strong in a way we barely understand. He added up. He got results.

So, please be absolutely clear – meditation isn't about withdrawing from the world, and it's not incompatible with being a very forceful presence there. In fact, it's what makes you able to be so effective, and so tireless. It especially means that you have no enmity, you do not divide, but always seek to win others over by your openness.

*Every river, every tributary, every tiny creek
is so distinctive that the salmon can smell it
through a thousand miles of ocean. But a
river surely feels joy to be back in the sea.*

MEDITATION – A SIMPLE GUIDE

Darren is sixty-nine, but he still has that trim and fit look of a soldier, though he hasn't been one for forty-five years. He is seated with crossed legs, his hands resting on his thighs and his back straight. His eyes are closed and his deeply lined face is relaxed.

It wasn't always that way; after returning from Vietnam, he drank so heavily that his first marriage ended and he was homeless for a time. He stabilized somewhat and remarried, then it all came back; he was suicidal and in and out of psychiatric treatment. His second wife and three stepchildren stood by him, and psychologists and an array of medications kept him coping, but only just. Then one day a group of veterans he belonged to attended a meditation course. It wasn't a sudden cure, but it clearly was a help, and that effect was cumulative. The active yoga, combined with mental tools to ease the waking nightmares in his mind, drew him and his mates into a whole different way of life.

I meet people with this kind of story all the time. A young mother with chronic back pain who tells me, 'I couldn't live if it weren't for meditation.' A teenage girl who uses it to combat intense anxiety and is helping her friends to learn it as well. Primary school children who meditate in the classroom and find it the best part of their school day.

Meditation is a word so often heard that we think we know what it is, even as we decide it's not for us! It has migrated from being a practice of monks and nuns in monasteries to a very widespread technique taught by psychologists as a first-line treatment.

In 1975, Herbert Benson, a professor of medicine and cardiologist, wrote a breakthrough book, the first describing meditation in simple terms for a Western audience. He called it *The Relaxation Response*, and perhaps that remains the very best term, because it emphasizes the goal. The relaxation response is a state your body goes into when your brain, essentially, stops stirring it up.

Our brains are amazing things. They are time travellers – not only can they remember experiences from long ago, they can also imagine future possibilities in great detail too. It's wonderful, but also a huge problem. Left to itself, your brain will ramble about, trying to win long-ago arguments, avoid looming disasters that may never happen, and getting annoyed about things in which you have no say.

The problem with this is that the emotional areas of our brain cannot distinguish if something is real or imagined. If you merely imagine sucking on a lemon, your mouth will pucker and dry. If you imagine a long-ago argument, or insult, your adrenaline will flow and your blood pressure rise. In short, your monkey mind stresses your body by telling it scary stories almost all the waking day. This can keep you in permanent anxiety mode.

Meditation is the method that very wise people devised to stop your mind bothering your body. Even happy thoughts carry a certain degree of tension and stress, and so we can never be fully calm while we are still thinking. In meditation, you *give your brain something harmless to do*, rather like giving a child a toy to play with while you speed past the ice-cream shop.

Too much mystery has been built around meditation, as with all things spiritual. If you were to sit in a warm spot in the sunshine, looking over a garden or a view of the sea, or even just by your fireside at home, you would eventually stop thinking and begin to calm down. You would finish with old arguments, let go of fears for the future, and peace would find you. Meditation is simply a trick for getting there straight away. Of course, once begun, it becomes a journey to very deep places, and brings moments, at least, of the complete loss of self, and a loving merging with the world that overcomes all ego and all fear.

The easiest and best way, taught all over the world, is simply to sit somewhere comfortable and count your breaths, in and out, while paying attention to how your breathing feels as you do so. It needs a gentle but patient attitude, as you will wander off within seconds, so you just need to quietly start again. That's all it is!

Within a minute or two, once you acquire the knack, the relaxation response simply arrives in your body. You will experience a lovely softening of your muscles and a falling away of outer worries and concerns. Breathing will become a kind of sensuous thing, rolling in waves, up and down your torso. Once it arrives, enjoy it for as long as you can spare.

What is happening is that your mind and body are entering a reset, and as your day unfolds, the effect will carry, and improve what happens. The effect might last half an hour, or come and go, or last all day. Meditation is filling your relaxation tank, ready to use later. The point of it is in how it changes the rest of your day. We all lose it eventually, but you can do 'spot' meditations during the day to restore it. Stuck at a traffic light, waiting in a bank, listening to a boring friend! The relaxation response is like a butterfly that you are luring to land on your shoulder; you can't make it, but if you are still enough, land it will.

Here's how I do it. (I'm a basket case in terms of a twitchy mind, and so, if I can do it, then you can too.)

I sit somewhere quiet: on a garden seat in my back paddock, or, if it's cold, on a rug beside the window where the sun first appears at my house. It can be an armchair in a hotel room, or anywhere, really. It helps to have your back straight. If you can manage sitting cross-legged on a cushion, that is probably ideal, because it says to your body, 'I am meditating now'. In this position, it's possible to sway a little bit to and fro and side to side; it's soothing and makes you more aware of your body.

Once in place, I run through a small sequence to help me 'arrive'. I listen for sounds far away – birds singing or a lawn-mower, or traffic in the distance. I just give each of these a few seconds of attention, then move lightly on. Then some sounds closer by – perhaps the hum of a fridge, or the wind in the eaves of the house. Then I arrive close up, right here, in my body.

Eric Harrison, who in his books and his teaching loves to make things simple and non-mystical, suggests having two or three big long sighs. (Do let people in your house know that's what you are doing, though, or they might think you are clinically depressed!) This seems to cue your body to start its calming journey. It's also a bit funny, which doesn't hurt. Some people make an 'om' sound three times, which is nice in the way it makes your brain vibrate a little.

Then the meditation proper. You begin to count your breaths. One. And. Two. And . . . Just breathe normally, and when you get to three, start again.

Most books suggest counting to ten or fifty, and for years I felt terribly inadequate because, by the count of two, my mind had already started to stray. I told Eric about this and he grinned and said, 'You know what? For ten years, I never could get past six!'

So I aim for three. The thing is, *it doesn't matter*. Nothing about meditation is to do with achievement or beating yourself up. The only attitude to ever take is one of gentle kindliness towards yourself. Well, there you went off on a wild sexual fantasy for three minutes, that's fine. The good thing is you noticed. Never hassle yourself about it, just gently start over. There is a trick that really helps: as you pay attention in detail to the muscles doing the breathing in and breathing out, you will notice the point where you change from out- to in-breath, and that it's quite a subtle thing. Your chest and belly have their own kind of sequence for turning round the direction of the breath. By noticing this, it engages your attention, and you stay in the moment more and more.

Your mind will jump about, but your deeper self – your heartbeat, and subtler things like blood pressure and immune response – will start to steady and ease. The relaxation response, as it kicks in, is exactly that: your breathing becomes really smooth, rolling, soft and deep; you feel warm and peaceful; you feel like you are being rocked in the arms of a loving parent. Okay, I am going on a bit, but trust me, it's nice.

That's the place you are headed for. Even just a moment or two of that is good. The aim of meditation is not the meditation itself, but the effects of it to improve the rest of your day. It will tend to last at least for a while, more as you get more aware. It will make your reactions less edgy or rushed. One effect I really love and find so helpful is that it seems to slow down time, so that you will have more time to consider your words, notice your inner reactions and a gap where you can choose what you do or say. A slight distance from the dramas and flickering trivia around you. You will be more tolerant and kindly towards yourself and others. The thing is, this is your natural state, this is *you with the stress taken away*. It's simply that, in modern life, we are over-revved nearly all the time, and have come to think that's how it must be. Meditation is getting back to how our bodies and brains are supposed to work.

There is one more thing: the ability grows. Each second you practise coming back, you are building the neuroplastic pathways towards being present. They will get stronger. Even noticing the touch of your hand on the doorknob as you leave your house, or the warmth of the sudsy water in the sink, you will begin to retrain your brain in presentness. It's always worth doing.

Meditation will become your friend, and a remedy for everything that life can throw at you. A kind of mental ju-jitsu to throw pain and difficulty over your shoulder and leave you happy and at peace.

Almost everyone who starts to meditate notices a disturbing thing; their brain behaves like a deranged monkey, racing into the forest of old regrets or arguments, thickets of memory – good and bad – or leaping about on the cliffs of future concerns. Or worse, it just goes to your shopping trip and what to cook for dinner. Or what someone said on Facebook. It isn't that meditation is causing such agitation, but simply you are getting a sudden window into what your brain does all the time!

None of this mental leaping about is of any help to us, either to our peace of mind or, just as importantly, to our effectiveness. And it certainly doesn't bring us joy. The only joy we ever have is now. And the only love we ever have is now. (In fact, the very definition of love, how you know it exists, how you feel it, is when you have someone's absolute attention.) And finally, the only impact we ever have is now. So we must make it count.

You, dear reader, may have a family to care for, and which needs you to be organized and to attend to it almost every waking moment. You may have a job that demands much of you. You might be dealing with tough things in your personal life that preoccupy and assail you. Talk of living in the present moment sounds about as helpful as advising you to take a month off on a desert isle.

But it is useful even just to nibble at the edges of this idea. For one thing, have you noticed that sometimes lately you make errors – lose your keys, cut yourself in the kitchen, trip or slip and hurt yourself, dent your car, forget something important that disrupts your whole day? Worse still, that your interactions with important people – kids, partner, relatives, business associates – are increasingly jangled and don't go well? Being here and now isn't all dreamy. It's about getting things right, by really attending to them well. Helping a child with five minutes of absolute attention might prevent months of them recovering from making a bad choice.

The present is a really important place. You can be present even in the melee of life, like a samurai in combat. Absolutely there, absolutely focused, absolutely and paradoxically calm. Making just the right action, in just the right second. You have met this: the doctor who takes their time with you and works out exactly what is wrong; the lover who is pure attention, gentle and deeply connecting with you. You've been in this place, just not very often.

Learn to be present and your life will work. Don't despair at how difficult that might sound because you've simply never been shown how. The ability to feel all your senses and be fully here is like a muscle within which you can build strength, a neural pathway that you can widen and grow. Do this more of the time and it will come more easily. Presence is a distinctive attribute that has always been acknowledged – 'she has such presence' – and is an idea as old as time. People will start to notice it about you. You will find relationships more sparky, jobs easier to do, mistakes less common. If you are seeking a partner, you will start finding that potential partners are much more attracted to you. There is nothing sexier – or winning – than having someone's full attention. So hopefully this has gained yours!

The pathway in your brain from distraction back to awareness can be practised almost anywhere. That feeling of calm is like coasting your engine back to idle, like snowflakes falling inside your body, all your muscles letting go. Life revs us up and up and up, we need to take ourselves back down as soon as the chance occurs.

Thich Nhat Hanh recommends starting with building present awareness – mindfulness – into small tasks. He suggests you choose these as daily rituals, making it habitual and refreshing in the course of your day. Doing the dishes. Brushing your teeth. Drying yourself after your shower. Simply pay attention to the senses, the warmth of the soapy water, the texture of your towel, and, if you can, dry yourself with more tenderness, slowly, with pleasure. These moments stolen from the tumult and race going on around you (which the consumer culture so wants you to keep engaging with) become precious small havens that you gradually expand to liberate the whole of your life.

The Four-Storey Mansion will always help you to get through the toughest times, the boring times, the confusing times. Its primary rule is to go down to the ground floor first. Notice the sensory details, both outside you in what you are touching, seeing and hearing, and on the inside of you, the small tingles and cascades, aches and strains, muscle actions and skin responses. Do this casually, when you remember, and just for a moment or two. That's when you will notice what needs to be changed or adjusted. Long enough to notice that this moment is unique, that this time you latch the door, or stop at a traffic light is not like any other. You are not even the same you; each time is different.

What you are doing each time you return to the present is building neural change. Spirituality is like a muscle you can strengthen. You are incrementally building a superhighway in your own neuroplastic brain, away from monkey madness distraction to being present. Until it becomes first nature. Of course, go on meditation retreats, walk the Camino de Santiago if you want to, it still comes back to this: knowing how to be here.

And for attitude, try gratitude. You have eaten good food and have hot water to wash with. You have your own teeth! (Remember those personal ads? 'Man, 61, seeks woman, view marriage, own teeth. It wasn't entirely clear if he was referring to himself, or his intended!) You are safe, your bed is warm. Notice that and be grateful. Thank you, clean hotel room. Thank you, aircraft landing safely. Thank you, familiar old teapot. Thank you, sunlit kitchen window.

By turning things that you have to do anyway into a ritual of returning to the present moment, it begins to avalanche – you want to be there all the time. You soon become intolerant of the rushed and jangled half-aliveness that used to be your life. You just won't do it anymore.

You'll also take yourself more lightly. The much-loved Canadian poet Alden Nowlan became very sick in his forties, and after months of unsuccessful treatment, on the brink of his life coming to an end, he was drawn to the ocean. So he went and lived in a cottage right on the shore. He spent hours every day just gazing at the water and the distant islands, and the clouds and birds as they came and went. It made him feel, he said, that everything was eternal, and that he really didn't matter that much, and this thought brought him a great deal of peace. And then he got well.

HOW TO KNOW SOMETHING WILL GO WRONG

I made a remarkable discovery a couple of years ago (I'm a slow learner). Every time – literally every time – I do something in order to 'get it over with' – because it's boring, because I am in a hurry, because it has to be done before I can get on with more important or enjoyable things – the same thing happens. It goes wrong!

Sometimes slightly but maddeningly wrong. Sometimes dropped-the-bolt-into-the-engine wrong. Trip-to-the-hospital wrong. When doing a task, but wishing the task was already finished, you can rely on it taking longer or needing to be done again.

Since 80 per cent of life is doing things that we might call boring, unproductive or trivial (but that just have to be done), each day is rife with opportunities for 'inattention stuff-ups'. I've not stopped to take off a hot sweater because it would slow me down digging a patch of garden! I was so 'not there' that I didn't notice I was hot. But I sure noticed how much I hated the digging. This is the kind of craziness no other animal would ever get into. One Buddhist tale tells of a man beside a forest path, sweatily and noisily trying to chop down a tree. His axe is so blunt, though, that it just bounces off. A concerned passer-by sees this and points it out to him. 'I don't have time for that,' the man explodes. 'Get out of here!' (In a sense, this whole book could be summed up in just four words. 'First, sharpen your axe.')

I am sure, dear reader, you never need this advice, but, for me, it helps to notice when I want a job to be over. To notice that this generally makes me do it badly, possibly seriously so. The key is to change gear and do the job with enjoyment and care. The destination is the grave – don't hurry to get there.

Toughening Up

The final thing to realize about spirituality is that it is tough. It isn't for wimps. People used to live on Atlantic islands in stone huts to pursue it. Jesus worked out his destiny while starving in the scorching wilderness. (And when the time came, he walked towards his own annihilation, standing up to the economic power of Rome and the spiritual betrayal of the priesthood.) Gandhi, Martin Luther King, Dietrich Bonhoeffer and Sophie Scholl, and millions of unsung leaders for change just like them, knew that their spirituality would put them in immense danger.

This was also the spirit of the world-famous 'tank man' who was photographed blocking a column of huge tanks near Tiananmen Square, at the time of the dreadful massacre there. His identity and fate may never be known, but he decided that something mattered more than his own life. It must have been a glorious feeling.

Spirituality is tough because it is preparing you for the toughness of life, what it will inevitably bring. Read this poem by Jeff Foster:

You will lose everything.
Your money, your power, your fame, your success,
    perhaps even your memories.
Your looks will go.
Loved ones will die.
Your body will fall apart.
Everything that seems permanent is impermanent and
    will be smashed.
Experience will gradually, or not so gradually, strip away
    everything that it can strip away.
Waking up means facing this reality with open eyes and
    no longer turning away.

But right now, we stand on sacred and holy ground, for
    that which will be lost has not yet been lost, and
    realising this is the key to unspeakable joy.
Whoever or whatever is in your life right now has not yet
    been taken away from you.
This may sound trivial, obvious but really knowing it is the key
    to everything, the why and how and wherefore of existence.
Impermanence has already rendered everything and
    everyone around you so deeply holy and significant
    and worthy of your heartbreaking gratitude.

Loss has already transfigured your life into an altar.

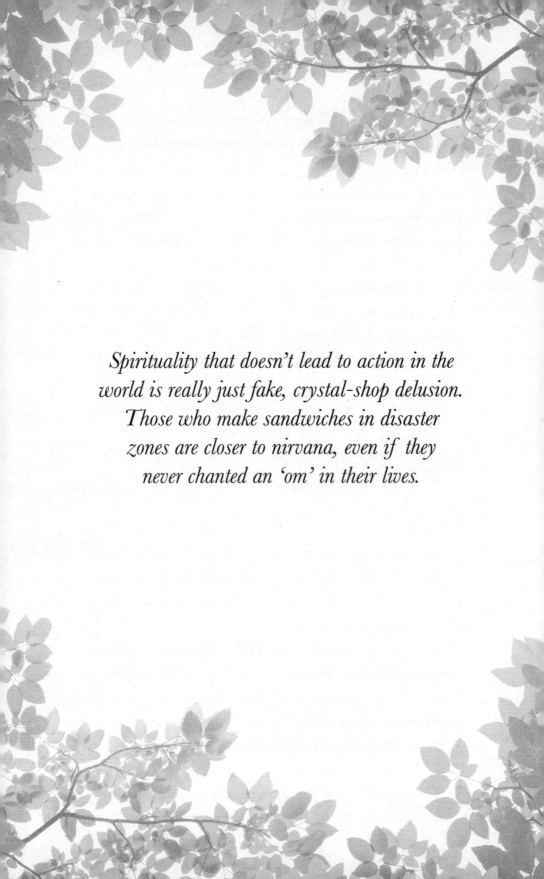

Spirituality that doesn't lead to action in the world is really just fake, crystal-shop delusion. Those who make sandwiches in disaster zones are closer to nirvana, even if they never chanted an 'om' in their lives.

Can you hear/see/feel what he is saying? Get ready to lose everything you love. That's what life does. But then *do something with that knowledge*. Meditate on the proximity, every second, of loss, destruction and the death of all you care about, and the result will take care of itself. You won't have to fake it. An intensification of your sense of the preciousness, the sacredness, of what now surrounds you – your imperfect spouse, your struggling kids, your own ham-fisted life, and the entire natural world wheeling around and above you – all becomes clear. All becomes luminous and perfect. You wouldn't want it any other way.

Just One More Thing

Many people make two big mistakes about spirituality: they think that it is merely a personal thing, and that its goal is to transcend ordinary life. This is a terrible misunderstanding, and it leads to monks in golden temples surrounded by poverty and injustice.

Personal bliss is a by-product, but it is not the goal of spirituality. In fact, it's the very opposite. You put your roots deep in the ground for only one reason – so that you can reach your branches high and stand against the storms. And thus you shelter the life around you, alongside you. Trees, as we now know, are life protectors for the rest of the ecosystem. How cool to be a tree kind of person! (Instead of just some cabbage.)

Knowing that you are part of everything means that you care about everything. If somewhere in the world a child is in agony and terror, then you cannot ever be at peace. You are unified, you are in a timeless transcendent calm, but you don't stop caring. You keep looking for ways to make the world right. Spirituality that does not lead to action is really fake, crystal-shop delusion. And those who make sandwiches in disaster zones are further on their way to God, even if they never chanted an 'om' in their lives.

The fourth floor opens to the sky. It can't help but put your smaller concerns into perspective. And in doing that it frees you to take enormous risks, make sacrifices, be extraordinarily brave. As the advent of parenthood makes the quietest mother or father into a ferocious beast in defence of their child, brotherhood and sisterhood with the living universe can release the most remarkable energies and powers. Perhaps we humans can stop being feedlot animals and finally be something more magnificent. Perhaps we can become, at last, fully human.

SPIRITUALITY REFLECTION EXERCISES ONE TO FIVE

1. Before reading this book, would you have said there was a spiritual dimension in your life?
2. If you answered no, then, from the wide-ranging list of activities we gave at the start of this chapter, would you now reconsider that you may in fact be a person who has spiritual practices as a core part of your life and your wellbeing?
3. When or where do you most feel the softening of your usual boundaries, and a joyful merging with the wider universe? This chapter argues that spirituality is the keystone or deep operating system of our human mind. That, without it, we just don't work.
4. Have you noticed that a spiritual sense changes and over-writes your other priorities or solves difficulties that occur on other levels of your mind? And on your life?
5. Have you glimpsed an aliveness sometimes in your life that you would like to have every day?

Happiness comes and goes, but deep peace builds and strengthens, and we can absolutely work on that.

9

Being Fully Human

We've covered a lot of ground in this book. Perhaps too much. Forgive me for this, I was desperate to pour out all that I could give you that might help. This closing section of the book appropriately merges all that we have learned about supersense and the Four-Storey Mansion to help you find freedom from the slavery of our times, and build a saner life and a saner world.

Let's start by asking you a simple question: what would it take for you to be happy? One way to answer this would be to finish this sentence: I will only be really happy when . . . You might have a single answer, but for many people there is a whole list. It's worth writing this list down some time, and noticing how that feels to see the race you have set yourself!

Most people's answers will naturally tend to arise from their stage of life. So you might find them saying:

. . . when I find a great partner and get married.

. . . when I find a decent job.

. . . when I escape my unhappy marriage.

. . . when the house is paid for and we can have a
    proper holiday.

. . . when my kids all finish university.

. . . when I can retire and my life is my own.

. . . when we solve the problem of climate change.

. . . when I win the lottery!

And some will depend on unique circumstances:

. . . when my daughter stops taking drugs.

. . . when my husband gets out of prison and gets his life
    on track.

. . . when my partner recovers fully from the cancer she
    is being treated for.

Once these conditions have been met, we tell ourselves, we can finally breathe easily and enjoy life. Who could blame the parent of a dangerously ill child for almost literally holding their breath, suffering terrible worry and grief, until they know their little one is well again? Even with more everyday goals – to find love, make a career, become financially secure – which almost everyone aspires to, it seems to make sense that we keep our efforts focused on the goal.

But there is another view on all of this. Long ago, while travelling in the US, in a small bookshop in Colorado, I found a postcard which I still have with me today. It is a photo taken through the window of an old cabin, bare-timber window frame thrown open, precipitous mountains outside which could only be the Himalayas, and some small flowering plant clambering up the wooden planking. And it reads: 'There is no way to happiness. Happiness is the way.'

Happiness is the way? It's an idea that your supersense grasps in a second, and your logic struggles with at first. So let's get into that struggle. I have friends from West Africa who never, in their culture, merely say 'goodbye'. They say, 'See you again, God willing.' It's so automatic, in that fraught and dangerous place, to make everything tentative, to take nothing for granted. But the odd thing is, these friends are the most laughing, exuberant and uninhibited people I know. Do they know something about how to thrive and fight on? Systemic racism, inequality, environmental disasters unfolding globally – all make the lives of billions of people fraught and terrible. We urgently need to face and fight these things. But what if joyfulness is the way we could be, even while doing this? What if the cart really does come before the horse? What if, in fact, this is the very secret of being able to keep going?

Most humans through history understood this; the idea of delaying happiness is not natural to human beings. It was built on the distorted versions of Christianity that sprang up in feudal times, the idea of a distant heaven, portrayed in the future, so that servitude and poverty in the present would be tolerated. Of 'pie in the sky when you die.'

Contemporary philosophers and psychologists now seriously

question 'the pursuit of happiness' as a worthwhile goal, because we now recognize that it's in the nature of emotions to be fleeting. Happiness matters, but you can't catch it; like the butterfly, it will come and sit on your shoulder. It's a matter of grace. We want something more solid and deeper, a contentment and sense of purpose that transcends how things are going right this minute. Who wants their inner peace to be a roller coaster?

Dietrich Bonhoeffer was a young German pastor in World War Two, who escaped the Nazis and fled to the United States, but he felt so bad to have abandoned his fellow countrymen and women that he returned and organized a resistance movement. Eventually and inevitably, he was arrested and imprisoned, and just days before the war ended, he was killed. In his writings and letters, it's very clear he was at peace and felt deeply 'right' about the course his life had taken. He was not made of different stuff to you or I, rather, he had figured something out. Deep down, what we truly want is to be 'lined up'. Having all of the levels of our Four-Storey Mansion pointed in the same direction – our actions, our feelings, our thinking and logic all pointing the same way – gives us a deep feeling of wellbeing. It's the 'way' – the sense of being on the right path. Happiness comes and goes, but deep peace builds and strengthens, and we can absolutely work on that.

Our ancestors for millions of years did not conceive of progress, did not see life as an upward race but as beautiful in itself.

They knew that life was a circle. Nature itself so clearly teaches this: spring always follows winter, and autumn summer; the sun and moon come and go; old people pass away, babies are born. If I have a single regret, it is that I've spent too much of my life speeding to some imagined goal, fretting over false urgencies, and I have missed so much happiness and connection on the way. As an old man, I now am letting go of this. Fear of old age, illness and death ripple through me, but today I sit watching the children play, and birds swoop over my head. My trees will blossom long after I am gone. 'Life going on' is good in itself. It's more than enough. It's a quiet ecstasy even to be fleetingly part of it.

WHAT THE RESEARCH SAYS

Happiness is now a major field of psychology research. And what researchers into happiness have established is that being happy or unhappy is not related to circumstance at all (once basic needs are met). It's actually a character trait. In other words, a habit of mind. We each have happiness default settings, and these are remarkably impervious to the facts of our lives. A grouchy person who wins the lottery will be back to being grouchy within a few hours. Probably about their tax bill! A cheerful person may find their car dinged in the car park and just put it down as 'one of those things'. If their house burns down, they'll be briefly quite upset (following our guidelines to let our feelings out), but will soon be cracking on with genuine optimism and perspective.

It's been said that getting married will make you happy for a week; a new car, for a weekend. A new TV, computer, fridge or lounge suite, for a couple of hours. Then you go back to your default position!

Again, test this against your experience. Most of us know people who just are happy. We love to be around them. They aren't faking it, it's not a brittle kind of brightness that is all facade. It's not whistling in the dark. They genuinely are upbeat, and are always giving things a try, being themselves, not worrying too much, not giving a damn about things that don't matter. How do they do that?

My only sister was called Christine, and she was gentle and loved handmade things, animals, children and being in nature. She had multiple sclerosis from her early thirties until she died at the age of sixty. She managed to raise two kids on a small hobby farm and live a remarkable life, though it was only with massive support from her community and Australia's pretty good and mostly free health system, and she was lucky in her choice of husband as well. Her life was tough, though, and in the end she told me she was keen to be through with it and die; she had grown tired of being so very disabled. But her demeanour for thirty years was not at all self-pitying. She would answer honestly about how she was, but would soon shift the focus to asking how your life was, and was such a sympathetic listener that you ended up telling her all your troubles. She was like this with pretty much everyone. Somewhere along the way, she had chosen her happiness setting, and it was realistically upbeat. Her life was, consequently, a beacon.

A Culture Off the Rails

We each have unique histories, and it takes individualized care to find what has harmed us. The misconceptions and the needless self-limitations we learned in childhood have to be rooted out so we can finally be free.

But not all misconceptions and limitations are personal. What if our whole society, the culture we've built up over hundreds of years, has its own inbuilt neurosis, a fundamental 'wrong take' on the answers to life? So that billions of people have been led down a wrong track, to needless suffering. A culture, too, can be traumatized, and can wander away from sanity and balance. And ours certainly has. The biggest collective delusion of the globalized world today is a misguided idea of how happiness can be found.

Here is the delusion in four easy steps:

1. There is a place called happiness.
2. It's in the future.
3. If you hurry, if you work hard, if you get ahead of everyone else, you can get there.
4. It's worth sacrificing almost everything in life to reach this destination, because, once you get there, your problems will be over.

I would guess that at least 75 per cent of people subscribe to this story and try to live it all their life. It's the central myth of Western civilization. And, of course, it's utterly wrong.

We desperately need to change this lie on which our society is based. Millions of people will work their entire lives doing things they pretty much hate, and not doing things they would really love, because they have a goal that is a big bank account, a fancy house, a big round-the-world trip or a retirement free of anxiety. Or some combination of all those. And they miss out on their present.

Few have explained this phenomenon as well as the incomparable teacher Alan Watts. For a generation growing up in the 1950s and '60s, Watts' books provided the most accessible bridge between the philosophies of East and West. And he pinpointed a central difference between the two. In the old East (very differently to today), life was not always seen as a line, but as a circle. Confucianism, Taoism and Buddhism all emphasized a life of simplicity, because it made one free. When the Emperor heard rumours of a remarkable philosopher called Chuang Tzu, he sent a deputation thousands of miles to invite him to the Imperial Palace. Chuang Tzu listened to their summons quietly and politely. Finally, he spoke, his voice almost a whisper. 'I have heard,' he said, 'that the Emperor keeps a two-hundred-year-old tortoise in a wooden box.' And he smiled, and that was the end of that.

In one of his most popular talks, Coincidence of Opposites, Alan Watts set out to describe how the universe works, which is essential knowledge if we are to successfully live there. The voice is BBC English, resonant and deep, but teasing, kindly . . .

'Existence, the physical universe, is basically playful.
There is no necessity for it whatsoever. It isn't *going*
anywhere; that is to say, it doesn't have some destination that it ought to arrive at. But it is best understood
by analogy with music. Because music as an art form
is essentially playful; we say "you *play* the piano," you
don't *work* the piano.
Why? Music differs, say, from travel. When you travel you
are trying to get somewhere . . .
In music, though, one doesn't make the *end* of a composition the point of the composition. If that were so, the
best conductors would be those who played fastest
and there would be composers who wrote only finales.
People would go to concerts just to hear one crashing
chord, because that's the end! Say, when dancing, you
don't aim at a particular spot in the room; that's where
you should arrive. The whole point of the dancing is
the dance.'

At this point in Watts' lecture, one could easily wander off
somewhere quiet, just to think about these questions. What
does this mean for my life? Have I forgotten to play, to dance?
And is he saying that all life should be like a dance, with no
end point in mind? Or is it just a message to have more fun?
(So you can get back to work refreshed.) Of course, dancing
does have a goal – it's got beauty and movement, and it's done
in harmony with music and a partner, and it promotes health
and longevity, and there is a kind of social purpose to this, to

kind of let go, to be part of a rhythm with either oneself or hundreds of other people. It's not goalless, but is somehow focused on the process and not something that comes at the end. Watts isn't arguing here for chaos, for structureless living. Dancing is a discipline, but it's also about letting go. Making love is dancing. Conversation is dancing. Gardening is dancing. Parenthood is dancing. Designing a car, or a city, leading a nation to peace and harmony. Now we are getting somewhere.

We interrupted Mr Watts in full flight, though. He isn't finished. He now does something very consequential for how we go about our lives, especially for those of us raising kids. He describes the process of indoctrination, of the mass hypnosis of children that takes place through their schooling and career progression, and the terrible effects of that.

> 'But we don't see that [playful nature of existence] as
> something brought by our education into our everyday
> conduct. We've got a system of schooling which gives a
> *completely* different impression. It's all graded. And
> what we do is we put the child into the corridor of this
> grade system with a kind of, "C'mon kitty, kitty, kitty!"
> And now you go to kindergarten, you know? And that's
> a great thing because when you finish that you get into
> first grade. And then – c'mon! – first grade leads to
> second grade, and so on, and then you get out of grade
> school and you go to *high* school, and it's revving up –
> the thing is coming! – then you're going to go to
> college, and by Jove then you get into graduate school,

and when you're through with graduate school you go out to join *the World*. And then you get into some racket where you're selling insurance, and they've got *that* quota to make. And you're going to make that. And all the time this *thing* is coming. It's coming! It's coming! That great thing, the success you're working for.

Then, when you wake up one day – about forty years old – you say, "My God, I've arrived! I'm *there*!" And you don't feel very different from what you always felt . . . Look at the people who live to retire and put those savings away. And then, when they're sixty-five, they don't have any energy left, they're more or less impotent, and they go and rot in an old people's – "*Senior Citizens*" – community. Because we've simply cheated ourselves the *whole* way down the line. We thought of life by analogy with a journey, with a pilgrimage, which had a serious purpose at the end and the thing was to get to that end. Success – or whatever it is, or maybe heaven – after you're dead. But we missed the point the *whole* way along. It was a musical thing and you were supposed to sing, or to dance, while the music was being played.'

And so he finishes, with that awful poignancy, 'while the music was being played'. Because one day it stops, and then it's too late. And the realization of that is the saddest thing in the whole of life. We chased the wrong things, and while we did, the ordinary but wonderful joys of our life – sunshine, flowers, animals, loving partners, children, friends, beaches – were all ignored or relegated to the gaps and small glimpses, to one day, when there's time. And we wasted our lives.

Just sit, for a time, with the grief of that. Is that true of you? Of people you have known? Your parents? Their parents? Your grown-up children? Is it true of the human race? And how would it be if we changed that?

'Ha!' you might say. 'If we all went off like hippies, nobody doing the work, nobody digging the minerals, building the cities, training the doctors, flying the planes, how long would your utopia last then? Who would feed you?' And that's fair enough. We don't have the vast herds of animals to eat, or the vast uninhabited landscapes to wander in, that our Cro-Magnon forebears had.

We have to shepherd our way out of the tangled wreckage of civilization with enormous care. But at least we can ease back on the headlong rush, the illusion that more will make us happier or safer. We can walk away from the excesses of our culture, and start to live on its margins, while we explore better ways. And while we do it, laugh in the sun, and love and cherish what is around us.

We can keep what is good and tune it down to something that can last. Ours is a civilization built on the horrific chaos and overload of more. We became numbed, so that only more can satisfy us.

This is what your supersense and your Four-Storey Mansion are telling you all the time – what you really want, what you really need. It's a superb guidance system. While writing this book, applying its lessons to myself, I have been dropping the urge to do so much. It's been an interesting time. What happens is that sometimes, following what my body seems to want, I sit almost motionless in my garden for uncounted periods of time, watching the birds and the sky. It just feels so good to do that, I am astonished. (I could take a holiday to the other side of the world, climb a mountain, visit a famous beauty spot, all highly approved-of activities in this culture, and still not feel this good.)

Sometimes I walk, or exercise, not to any programme or routine, but simply because it's what I feel like doing at that moment. My muscles seem to tell me – use us! The outdoors calls to me. Or the indoors, a book or a video. And guess what? Sometimes the urge to write and become super-productive, organized and energetic takes over, and I work hard for hour after hour, heedless of the time. That's what is happening as I write this. It's enormous fun. I hope it helps other people, but at least it helps me, and that's a start.

NOT EFFORTING IS ACTUALLY PRODUCTIVE

The experience of being in the present – even some of the time – is not that you find everything coming to a stop. It's as if suddenly, now that you are not blurring your life with speed, skimming the surface of your own existence, it becomes five times more intense. It's spicy and sweet, and poignant yet light-hearted, all at the same time. 'In the stillness is the dancing.'

Remember when you were first in love with someone, the very first time you actually touched – perhaps it was accidental – and it was just so electric? That was because you were absolutely 'there', you weren't thinking about anything else. That kind of intensity is always available to you. You can be in love with your life. Even the painfulness of life is still life, still the dance.

Stillness is like a fountain, things happen there. Annie Dillard wrote about this from another direction. She said to go and sit in nature. Be in a wild place. And something will always happen. It's the nature of creation that it goes on creating. Let it create you too.

If you abandon pressure on yourself, or on your child if you are a parent, it doesn't lead to disintegration. In fact, the opposite: it leads to a very grounded, creative and healthy kind of balance. Life is still lived. Just in a better direction. You find that you can still have intention and direction, but it is no longer forced. You dance with your life, and trust that inside you, inside your children, inside your partner, is a harmony and goodness. Some kids learn better without school. Plants grow without us pulling on their leaves. Even a few steps in this direction restore some sanity. In fact, that's the best way to progress.

Detuning from the life-destroying story of 'one day you will be happy' is not easy, but there are forces on your side, because you remain an animal and a superb body–mind system is working to help you. It's not so much a programme as a deep listening and following as your own brain, interacting with the world around you, begins to integrate itself.

Drop Out, Tune In

In the Covid virus shutdown of 2020/2021, when millions of people had to stay at home, something interesting started to take place. Cut off from the scurry of life in the big world, some people began to have rather a sweet time. I found this when I asked my worldwide Facebook communities of parents how they were faring. Some were having a terrible time because of the demands of their job, and kids, and the expectation that they would somehow turn home into an eight-hour classroom. But quite a large number found that they were enjoying it a great deal. Life was slower, their family was more connected, and time seemed to have a rhythm and flow it didn't usually have.

The key to this enjoyment seemed to be in letting go of the usual pressures – especially for their children to 'get ahead', not 'fall behind', or 'stay in the race'. Schools – the good, brave ones – were also saying this to the parents: 'The schoolwork

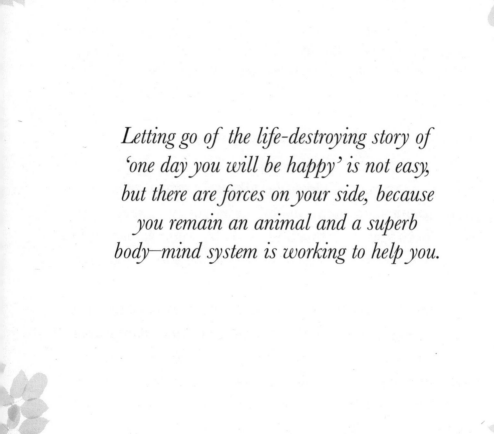

Letting go of the life-destroying story of 'one day you will be happy' is not easy, but there are forces on your side, because you remain an animal and a superb body-mind system is working to help you.

is not that important right now', 'Just do the essentials, give it an hour, two for teenagers'. It began a certain attitudinal shift that this letting go might be better for everyone's mental health and wellbeing, and that the things being 'learned while not learning' were more tangible, more consequential than the usual busywork of the curriculum. Things about life. Things that might help them actually have good careers, be creative and self-motivated adults. It was all very subversive.

One self-help strategy today, widely used, is a gratitude journal. One has to (grudgingly, I am sure) write five good things that you are grateful for at the end of each day, or on waking in the morning. It's pure and simple brain plasticity, noticing what you have, rather than what you don't, and, done sincerely, it quite quickly rewires you to a better outlook. (This is important, in a world bombarded by marketing, which aims to make you miserable with what you have by showing what you don't. It's programming you with discontent, if you let it.)

Happiness is, after all, only an emotion. It's the very nature of feelings to ebb and flow. And what's more, happiness arrives accidentally, as much as it does from plans made or conditions controlled. You hear this all the time: 'We had very little but we had more fun . . . when the kids were little . . . that time our holiday booking was all screwed up, so we just had to improvise'. Older people are very clear: 'I was happy then, and I didn't know it. I wish I could go back'. Since learning this, I have begun to train myself to know I am happy when it is actually happening – this is it! I am in bliss. I am walking down a country lane and the sun comes out through the clouds. My grandchild runs ahead of me across an open grassy ridge, birds wheeling overhead. Or after lovemaking, lying still, skin tingling and heart beating strongly, thinking, Okay, I could die right now! Be totally fine! I have to see the doctor tomorrow, but – that's tomorrow. The very real shadows across our lives just make it more intense. Forget about perfection, as you finally appreciate what is.

Pain is Part of It

Which brings us to the question of pain. How do we deal with it? And, since it can't be avoided, how can we at least not make it worse? In the 1970s, two American meditation teachers – Stephen and Ondrea Levine – did an astonishing thing. They created a free telephone service for people undergoing traumatic grief. They simply put a phone in and manned it themselves, as a form of service to the world. In their book *Meetings at the Edge,* they characterized the outcome of their collaborations with their callers as 'opening the heart in hell'. They believed, and found it to be true, that the most hostile and terrible circumstances were the very place where we had to abandon ourselves to tears, feel and release the rage, shudder with fear, and come out the other side, ready to love and be at peace. To use the Four-Storey Mansion, in other words.

One caller was a parent whose young adult daughter had been abducted, tortured and killed. They had suffered for years after this; they relived the details of their daughter's death thousands of times. Yet, gradually, talking to the Levines (and without them pointing it out, which would have been a terrible discounting of their pain), they became aware of a simple fact: that their daughter had gone through it only once. It was as terrible as one could imagine, but it was finite. Good parents empathize with their children, we put ourselves in their place continually as part of how we care for them. It was a natural trap to fall into. They were caught in reliving her last hours and minutes, somehow believing that this was what their love for her required. It was not helpful, it did not honour her, she would not have wanted that. They began to untie the bonds and grieve, and so be able to remember her happy, warm and alive.

We all of us will experience intense emotional pain many times as we make the journey from birth to death. To have happiness and joy, we must also have grief and sorrow. If we stubbornly refuse to grieve, we just get depressed.

Grief itself follows this wave-like pattern. We are designed to do it in manageable chunks. So many of my clients have described this. Devastated by loss, after a week or a month, they catch themselves laughing at a joke, or relishing some treat or experience that has come along. And suddenly they think, Is this okay? Am I allowed to laugh? To feel happy for a moment? Not only are you allowed to, it's the only way to ever heal. All you have to do is rise and fall over this wave. As psychotherapist Sheldon Kopp describes, 'We call out to God – why me? And God answers – why not?' And, a few pages later, 'You can SO stand it.'

THE PROM AND MR CALDWELL

When I was in Year 9 at school, a new maths teacher arrived, freshly graduated. Mr Caldwell was stern looking, but with a sense of fun just below the surface, and to our delight we landed him as our homeroom teacher as well.

At the first home-group meeting, he announced that, each week, one of us would be asked to tell the story of our lives to the class. And we did. It was a revelation to hear kids you had sat next to half your life telling things you'd never known. We started seeing each other as people!

That was only the beginning. He sent a letter home to everyone, saying that he would come and visit all thirty-five of us, and talk to our parents about our future plans. (The rumour went around that, with a visit from Mr Caldwell looming, some people redecorated their living room or bought a new lounge suite!) He then tested the whole class's IQ en masse, and this was what he took along to show parents. In those days, most kids left school at fourteen, and this was a very working-class school. Armed with the figures to prove it, he lectured parents that their daughter or son was university material, and they mustn't hold her back. She could be a doctor or a lawyer. This was gritty stuff – unheard of, really. Lives were changed.

Once, later in the year, some of my friends said they were going to visit his house, and off we went. We showed up on our bikes, and, to our amazement, found several of the kids who tended to struggle in class there (it was a Saturday morning), doing their homework, as if it was the most natural thing in the world. Mrs Caldwell, a relaxed and artistic-looking young woman, plied us with hot chocolate. We had never seen inside a teacher's house before – it was very avant-garde; a glimpse into the main bedroom revealed a nude painting above the bed!

Not stopping at that, it was announced around mid-year that we were to have a class camp at Wilson's Promontory, (or, the Prom, as we came to call it) a national park we had only heard of in surfie legend. Nobody did class camps in those days, we'd never heard of the idea. A carload of us had to go with Mr Caldwell and scope it out, on a long day's drive down. And I was one of the three invitees who crowded into his Mini Minor for the trip. The least extrovert, most unsocial kid in the class. It meant a lot.

Wilson's Promontory was to become my spiritual home, as life opened up, in late adolescence, when I found my tribe – Kombi-van loads of friends making the pilgrimage many times, winter and summer. The wide beaches, heath-covered rolling hills and granite peaks to climb, always in sight of the sea. It was a place that you found you belonged in the world. We honeymooned there.

In 2015, I went back there, on purpose, after many decades away. A pilgrimage. The night before arriving, I stayed in a cottage near the park entrance, taking it slow to absorb the emotions of coming home to a sacred place. The next morning, I set off into the park, with the radio playing in my rented car. ABC Radio was on, and I heard a man being interviewed about school leadership. I knew before they confirmed it at the end of the interview. It was Brian Caldwell. Now a professor of education. Taking me back to the Prom.

We Need Each Other

Self-help books often make the mistake – the deception, really – that we can do it on our own. But that was never how human beings were designed. We are a clan, not an individual; a lone human is not a functioning unit.

Sometimes, in fact surprisingly often, the pain of life is too much to face alone. It's the child inside us that feels things, and every child needs someone calm and strong to care and hold them through the worst. We need people, and that means being able and willing to trust at least a couple of people who can 'hold' the amount of feeling you are having, not panic, and not be so discomfited that they have to put up barriers.

No amount of academic training in psychology can give you this ability. But life certainly can. I used to tell my trainees, 'Unless you have suffered, you are not much use to anyone.' You have to know from the inside what real pain is like. (Many medical specialists we have encountered seem to lack this vital ingredient in their training, and it makes them heartless and arrogant, and being their patient a dehu-manizing ordeal, traumatic in itself.) Life is hard. The idea that one day everything will be okay is often simply not so, and we have to get used to that possibility and still be able to laugh and love in spite of it.

A famous American naval officer, James Stockdale, was imprisoned and tortured for over seven years by the North Vietnamese before finally being freed. James discovered the

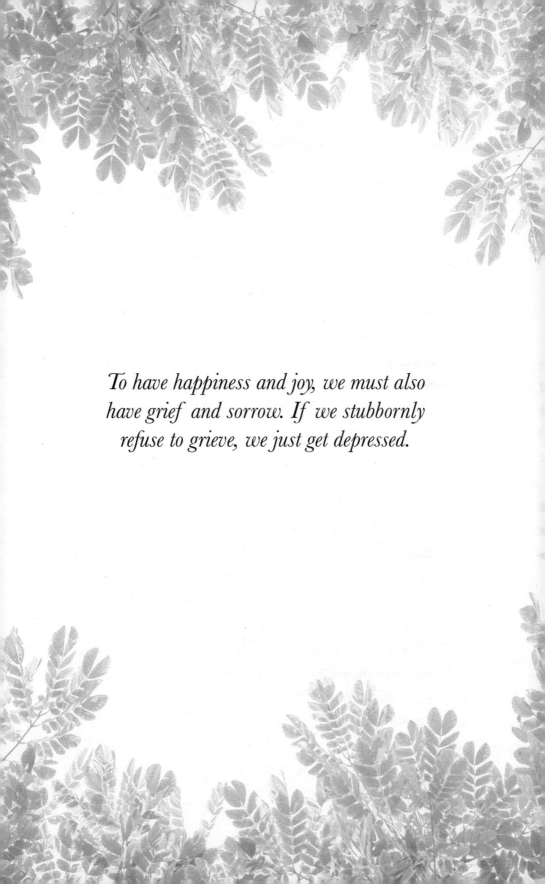

To have happiness and joy, we must also have grief and sorrow. If we stubbornly refuse to grieve, we just get depressed.

paradox that his fellow prisoners, who held out that 'it'll all be okay' viewpoint, 'we'll be out of here by Christmas, or Easter', did not do well. When those dates went past, they gave up hope, and, in the terrible conditions, they often died. James kept in his mind the possibility that he would never be released. Yet he did not give up on the will to survive, and working on that. He refused to let other people determine his state of mind. He is still alive today.

By following the ideas in this book, you can make a huge difference in your life, but will it end your problems? Probably not. (Perhaps you will have more worthwhile problems.) The more you love, the more you will grieve. The question is – can you live with an open heart, even though you know that? If you can, there will be plenty of joy. It's the way we are made.

The Four-Storey Mansion will get you there. Just move in. Move about. See if you can, as you walk through the journey of your days, be in your body. Listen to those micro-sensations that are your feeling reactions to everything around you. Let your heart experience the depths of sorrow and grief, shudder with fear sometimes and let it go. Feel righteous fury, then settle it into resolute patient action. Catch yourself being happy and feast there for a while. Think clearly and well. Keep noticing you are a brother or sister to every living thing – they love you, and they are you. The stars wove you and will take you back. We're all just the wind in the grass – no more, no less. It's the most beautiful thing.

Christine and Steve Howard, Tidal River Beach, 2010.

About the Author,

If You Want to Know

When you first begin to read a book, a quiet process starts to happen in your mind. Part of your brain tries to imagine the author, to 'suss them out'. Are they someone wise enough to learn from? Are they well motivated and genuine, or just 'out to make a quid'? A book is a kind of conversation, and you want to know who you are talking to. So here goes . . .

I'm a husband, dad and grandad. For many years, I worked around the world, but my home is a small community on the island of Tasmania. To a British reader, Tassie, as we call it, is rather like living in the 1950s, but with feminism and the Internet – so a pretty good place! It's quiet and slow, and so am I. I'm grateful to live where I can swim in the ocean and be out under big skies.

I was a psychologist for over forty years, working with people in sometimes terrible circumstances. The main thing I have taken from this work is admiration for my fellow human beings, seeing them overcome trauma and suffering, and still be kind-hearted and not give up.

My work has made me furious at the stupidity in the world, since that is what most evil stems from; but I have learned to hold firm to the joy and beauty within it, too, in order to continue the fight. In my professional and personal life, I have learned that trauma can destroy us, and it can turn us into destroyers of others. But it can also crack us open, 'opening our hearts in hell' so that we become more loving, and alive. Those who have come through a lot are often the ones who see the truth, and are not afraid to speak it. Recently, I chastised our (Australian) Prime Minister in the national press.[7] It caused some waves, but this is the task of old people. You have to live your values.

There is something else you should know. Several decades ago, I was talking with a psychiatrist friend over lunch. Mid-conversation, he asked me a series of questions. Then a concerned look appeared on his face. 'You do know, don't you? ', he said. 'You've got Asperger's?' And a silent avalanche began to swoop down through my memory banks.

Back in my 1950s childhood on the windy Yorkshire coast, this was a condition that nobody knew about. I just thought I was shy! As a little five-year-old boy, on my first day of school, I decided education wasn't for me, and I walked out of the school gate and went home. The look on my mother's face as I waltzed in the door was something to see.

Little boyhood is not that complicated – playing, shouting and running about – and I loved my life, back then. But, in the teenage years social skills mattered more, and I just couldn't get it right with people. I could see everyone doing this thing called 'conversation', and it looked like fun. At this age, the girls at school were like goddesses – a smile from one of them could really light up your day. But every attempt to connect with them just went astray. (Later, when girls did seem to like me, I just couldn't read their signals, and some very nice girls went unkissed!)

Life could have gone badly for me, as many young men's lives do, but for two things: I was raised by kind and loving – if somewhat bewildered – parents, and I had some exceptional teachers, youth workers and others who saw that I had a good heart, and they did their best to include me. When I looked like I was becoming homeless, they found me somewhere to live, and then later found me a job – working, incredibly, with troubled kids! Inspired by that, I returned to my studies and became a psychologist. If you, dear reader, are a teacher or social worker who cares for young people who don't fit in, then you are my people.

Psychology is a good career if you can't relate to human beings. Over time, I finally learned what most people just instinctively seemed to know: that conversation follows rules – like ping-pong or tennis, it goes to and fro. You say something, and then you wait for the other person to say something back. I hadn't known that! (Aspie people often sense a gap coming in the conversation, feel terrified, and then talk and talk and talk to fill it up.) And there are things called emotions – they show on people's faces and give you information about the state they are in, and how you might want to respond. (It's not only autistic people who have trouble with this.)

I knew that I had to learn – and learn fast, because every day in our waiting room were families in real pain, and kids whose lives were not headed for good places. I sought out the very best people, in the therapy world, and while my friends were buying houses and cars, I travelled repeatedly across the globe to sit at the feet of the masters. I found that I could take into my own sinews and bones and brain the attitudes and ways of being with people of these superb human beings. I didn't even understand it, but I could do it.

Finding the missing pieces of how to be fully human seemed to unleash something in me. Please don't hear this as boasting – I take little credit for this – but today I can stand in front of a thousand people in an auditorium and hold them spell-bound, and in fact that became my primary work. The half-dozen books I have written are in four million homes, and people seem to love them. I have travelled from being a lonely outsider to someone rather capable (though only in parts of my life, others are still quite hard).

I was convinced that people should not have to wait until they were in real pain, that much of what we were learning with families could be taught before marriages imploded or kids went off the rails.

The combination of writing and doing live presentations took me to so many countries and I met people in so many cultures, from hunter-gatherers to billionaire urbanites, in the worst of tragedies and to the most inspiring achievers. The topics I was interested in could be related to by everyone. I loved to listen and learn. I was the very opposite of an expert. And so real connection could be made. I had a recurring problem with taxi drivers bursting into tears!

My life these days has a new kind of freedom. Though it's shadowed somewhat by the approach of infirmity and death. That shadow is bracing. Last summer, I kayaked around a bend on a flooded river and saw ahead of me a fallen tree blocking the way. I frantically tried to turn away, but the current was too strong, and my kayak hit the trunk broadside. Within seconds, it was being sucked underwater, while I pulled my body weight up onto the branches. It happened too fast for me to be frightened. That only came afterwards, on my knees in a forest clearing, drenched to the bone, trying to push through dense scrub so I could walk out to a road and home. Knowing I needed to think calmly, I let my body shiver and shudder to release the tension of having almost drowned. My life since that day has a focus that it didn't have before.

This book is my attempt, while my brain still functions, to throw a lifeline to the human community that I loves so much, and so much want to thrive after I am gone. It's my personal attempt, really, to help to save the world.

Steve Biddulph

Notes, Sources and References

for Professionals and the Very Keen

The science of supersense is beautifully surveyed in Hodgkinson, Langan-Fox and Sadler-Smith, 'Intuition: A fundamental bridging construct in the behavioural sciences' (2008). Evans and Stanovich provide a further review of the evidence in *Dual Theories of Higher Cognition: Advancing the Debate* (2013).

More recent articles have continued to develop our understanding of how 'parallel processing' works. Shea and Frith (2016) use the term 'type 0 cognition', and describe it as 'characterized by automatic computational processes operating on non-conscious representations.' Which is a good reason for calling it supersense! There are also exciting side journeys emerging such as Brosnan, Lewton and Ashwin's article investigating parallel processing in people on the Autism spectrum.

The go-to person for psychotherapists interested in neuroscience, especially where it intersects with child development and attachment theory, is the legendary Allan Schore. Schore's book *Affect Regulation and the Origin of the Self: The Neurobiology of Emotional Development* (1994), remains the most astonishing synthesis of how we are put together, functionally and structurally, through the interaction of parenting and our growing mind. It is a very dense read, however, although gut feelings are covered throughout, including this excellent summation of how we come to lose touch with them (Schore, page 281). 'Deficiencies of reciprocal interactions within the mother-infant regulatory system can cause the child to fail to be "in tune" with himself. This growth inhibiting environment produces an individual with high levels of inhibited, repressed, and therefore unconscious affect. These experiences may interfere with the development of prefrontal autonomic control that is required *for the experiencing of visceral, interoceptive "gut feelings" in response to real and imagined threats.'* (Italics are mine). Andie, the young mother and GP in chapter one may have her parents to thank for her responsive interior signals, and the ability to respond to them. And so for being alive.

Schore has since written a series of follow-up books which are somewhat easier to read. The latest and most specific to our purpose here is the 2019 release *The Development of the Unconscious Mind*.

From a completely different quarter comes Eugene Gendlin, whose bestselling book *Focusing* (1982) broke the story on this whole new layer of being and learning, 'down below' our emotions. Gendlin is a professor of philosophy as well as a psychotherapist, and for him the mind-body question never existed. It's all one. Ann Weiser Cornell's simple manual, *The Power of Focusing* (1996), is a delightful workbook for either self-therapy or for therapists wanting to greatly deepen what they do. Nothing beats experiencing the person themselves, and you can readily Google presentations and even a demonstration or two by Gendlin. These are priceless glimpses of a human being who lived what he taught.

Gendlin's contemporary successor is a more familiar name to therapists, the concept of somaticization is not identical to Gendlin's felt sense, but is in the same direction. It is followed up empirically, and skilfully in Bessel Van Der Kolk's work, for example his 2015 book *The Body Keeps the Score: Mind, Brain and Body in the Transformation of Trauma*. Van Der Kolk offers excellent trainings easily found online. Gendlin, though, remains for me the most fertile source because as an academic philosopher he reaches into deeper water about what a human being actually is, especially that we are not as separate from all of life as we experience ourselves to be. This then underpins my chapter on spirituality, though of course it has also been implicit in Buddhism, and in Christian mysticism as well as many other faith traditions.

The injunctions which arise from traumatic or even normal childhoods in our culture were described in detail by my own teachers at the Western Institute for Group and Family Therapy, Bob and Mary Goulding, in *Changing Lives Through Redecision Therapy* (1997). Redecision is the mature and rational outgrowth of Gestalt therapy, yet loses none of its immediacy and energy, nor its capacity to neurally rewire traumatic childhood learning. The list of injunctions in the main text is incomplete; several more severe ones were beyond the scope of self-help settings.

But therapists are encouraged to read the full list in the Gouldings' own books, designed for professional use.

Writers as varied as Robert Bly and James Hillman, as far back as Carl Jung and as vibrant as Clarissa Pinkola Estés, have bemoaned modern humans' dwindling *interiority* – the wisdom and self-knowledge of our own inner processes. It's clear in reading them that we have not only an inner child, but an inner jaguar or brown bear (or hamster!), twitching with aliveness and hypersensitive perception of our environments, integrating and knowing a hundred times what our conscious mind can ever manage. And that's only the ground floor. A lack of interiority is disastrous for functioning well – we become robotic, a chaos of appetites and insecurities.

Yet, despite this, we all recognize wisdom and authenticity when we see it, and it's really not that hard to bring back to life.

The research into mortality following a bereavement is extensive, the most recent and proactive about what can be done to prevent it is King, Lodwick, Jones, Whitaker and Petersen, 2017. Here are a useful couple of sentences from the conclusion: 'A recent cohort study appears to show that depression mediates the relationship between bereavement and subsequent mortality most particularly in men. Grief counselling in the early months of bereavement, together with a more specific talking therapy for those with complicated grief, might play the greatest role in reducing this risk.'

Living in the present is wonderfully argued by Alan Watts in *The Wisdom of Insecurity* (1951). Rather quaintly to us, he described the late 1940s as an age of anxiety; heaven knows what he would have thought of the 2020s. Thich Nhat Hanh's book *The Art of Living* was my favourite source for his transformative ideas for activism based in self-forgetting. Here is just one quote: 'Happiness and peace are born from transforming suffering and pain.' This of course is the very opposite of what our culture believes. The dynamic nature of emotions – how it's in their movement that we find joy, and their healing that we find purpose – was of course the message of Buddha. And the message of Jesus (in his time a very radical one) was that we are in this life for each other, and – in the trenchant title of Mary Robinson's autobiography – *Everybody Matters*.

Detailed citations are here:

Bly, R., *A Little Book on the Human Shadow* (New York: Harper Collins, 1988).

Brosnan, M.,Lewton, M., and Ashwin,C.,'Reasoning on the Autism Spectrum: A Dual Process Theory Account', *Journal of Autism and Developmental Disorders* 2016 Jun;46(6):2115-2125. doi: 10.1007/s10803-016-2742-4.

Cornell, Ann Weiser, *The Power of Focusing: A Practical Guide to Emotional Self-Healing* (Oakland, CA: New Harbinger Publications, 1996).

Evans, B. and Stanovich, K. E., 'Dual-Process Theories of Higher Cognition: Advancing the Debate', in *Perspectives on Psychological Science*, Vol. 8, Issue 3, 2013, p. 223.

Foster, Jeff. *You Will Lose Everything* www.lifewithoutacentre.
    com/writings/you-will-lose-everything/

Gendlin, E., *Focusing,* (New York: Bantam Books, 1978).

Goulding, R. and M., *Changing Lives Through Redecision Therapy*
    (New York: Grove Atlantic, 1997).

Greig, A., *At the Loch of the Green Corrie* (London: Quercus, 2010).

Hanh, T. H., *The Art of Living* (London: Rider, 2017).

Hillman, J. and Ventura, M., *We've Had a Hundred Years of
    Psychotherapy and the World's Getting Worse,* (New York:
    HarperCollins, 1992).

Hodgkinson, G. P., Langan-Fox, J., Sadler–Smith, E., 'Intuition: A
    fundamental bridging construct in the behavioural sciences',
    in *British Journal of Psychology*, Vol. 99, Issue 1, 2008, pp.
    1–27.

Jockelson, D. davidjockelson.com

King, M., Lodwick, R.,Jones, R., Whitaker, H., and Petersen, I.
    'Death following partner bereavement: A self-controlled
    case series analysis.' *PLOS ONE* March 15, 2017. https://doi.
    org/10.1371/journal.pone.0173870

Matthiessen, P., *The Snow Leopard* (New York: Bantam Books,
    1978); *Nine Headed Dragon River* (Boulder, Colorado:
    Shambhala Publications Inc, 1987).

Pinkola Estés, C., *Women Who Run With the Wolves* (New York:
    Ballantine, 1992).

Payne, K. J. with Ross, L. M. *Simplicity Parenting* (Ballantine,
    2009)

Robinson, M., *Everybody Matters* (London: Hodder and Stoughton,
    2012).

Schore, A., *Affect Regulation and the Origin of the Self* (Hillsdale, NJ: Lawrence Erlbaum, 1994); *The Development of the Unconscious Mind*, (New York: Norton, 2019).

Shea, N., and Frith, C. 'Dual-Process Theories and Consciousness: The case for "Type Zero" cognition.' *Neuroscience of Consciousness*, Volume 2016, Issue 1, 2016, niw005, https://doi.org/10.1093/nc/niw005

Watts, A., *The Wisdom of Insecurity* (New York: Vintage, 2011, originally published New York: Pantheon Books, 1951); *The Tao of Philosophy*: Coincidence of Opposites

References

1 Award-winning journalist Madeleine Bunting wrote a wonderful book about this called *Willing Slaves: How the Overwork Culture is Ruling Our Lives* (London: Harper Perennial, 2005).

2 Stroebe, M., Schut, H., Stroebe, W., 'Health outcomes of bereavement', in the *Lancet*, December 2007, vol. 370 (9603), p. 1960–73.

3 Moon, J.R., Kondo, N., Glymour, M.M., Subramanian, S.V., 'Widowhood and mortality: a meta-analysis', in *PLoS ONE*, August 2011, Vol. 6(8), e23465.

4 In the US, there was no NHS or Medicare at that time, and so only well-off people or those in good jobs had secure health coverage.

5 This is a simplified version, the full version used in the study is at www.ajpmonline.org/article/S0749–3797(98)00017–8/ fulltext

6 This form of therapy was based in transactional analysis (TA). A forerunner of today's cognitive behaviour therapy, and in fact far superior to it, TA is based on uncovering the 'tape' collection of parental programming, and how it played out in our thinking and relating to others (hence the 'transaction'). But the Gouldings added the dynamic action-based methods of Gestalt therapy, which you could say was the forerunner of mindfulness therapy, but far more vigorous and intense, intended to forge new brain connections around long-held patterns of self-imitation and dysfunction.

7 Steve Biddulph, 'Morrison a "bad dad" for denigrating young climate protesters', in *Sydney Morning Herald*, 1 October 2019: https://www.smh.com.au/national/morrison–a–bad–dad–for–denigrating–young–climate–protesters–20190930–p52w63.html

Acknowledgements

First of all, to Carole Tonkinson, publisher at Bluebird Books, who was almost a co-author of the work. Carole knows this subject deeply and understood the scope of what was being attempted. She never hurried me. And, in an elegant cafe in London, she spoke those words all authors long to hear: 'Write what you want!'

Shaaron Biddulph weaves inextricably through everything I do. She has stuck with me since the very start, and both embodies and encourages full humanness. God bless you, Shaaron.

Sean Doyle of Lynk Manuscript Services wrangled the structure early on and is also a long-term student of spirituality and human growth. The book is lighter and clearer from his help, and his encouragement.

Alison Howard, Di Davies, Neil Shillito and Dean Yates read early versions and gave great help from their own deep thinking about life and suffering, joy and growth.

Ari Biddulph provided rapid and sharply evaluated research, across diverse fields of knowledge, with humour and perceptive commentary added. She is also a very inspiring and courageous human being.

Hockley Spare was a careful and supportive editor, who it was a joy to work with. Ingrid Ohlsson is my energetic Australian publisher at Pan Macmillan. People working in printing factories, paper recyclers, truck drivers, accountants, publicists and booksellers are usually overlooked, but not by me. Thank you for making all books possible.

Lyn Edwards got my body straight and added years to my life. I can't overstate the importance of this.

Helen Cushing taught me about the three states of mind, and a lot about meditation. Eric Harrison's books really helped too.

I have never met Helen Garner, but her storytelling, by its crispness, compassion and ability to never take comfort in judgmentalness, has influenced every Australian writer worth their salt.

For forty years, I followed my dimly felt supersense that something was missing from human psychology, and from the Western view of the mind. When I finally found that waterhole in the desert, the spirit of Eugene Gendlin was sitting there with his warm eyes and sharp intelligence. So, thank you to him, and the whole tradition of humanistic, caring, relational psychology, which is once again rising up to save us from the machinery of doom.

Index